100 Daily Prayers

For My Family

The quoted ideas expressed in this book (but not Scripture verses) are not, in all cases, exact quotations, as some have been edited for clarity and brevity. In all cases, the author has attempted to maintain the speaker's original intent. In some cases, quoted material for this book was obtained from secondary sources, primarily print media. While every effort was made to ensure the accuracy of these sources, the accuracy cannot be guaranteed. For additions, deletions, corrections, or clarifications in future editions of this text, please write Freeman-Smith.

Scripture quotations are taken from:

The Holy Bible, King James Version (KJV)

The Holy Bible, New International Version (NIV) Copyright © 1973, 1978, 1984, by International Bible Society. Used by permission of Zondervan Publishing House. All rights reserved.

The Holy Bible, New King James Version (NKJV) Copyright © 1982 by Thomas Nelson, Inc. Used by permission.

Holy Bible, New Living Translation, (NLT) copyright © 1996. Used by permission of Tyndale House Publishers, Inc., Wheaton, Illinois 60189. All rights reserved.

The Message (MSG)- This edition issued by contractual arrangement with NavPress, a division of The Navigators, U.S.A. Originally published by NavPress in English as THE MESSAGE: The Bible in Contemporary Language copyright 2002-2003 by Eugene Peterson. All rights reserved.

New Century Version®. (NCV) Copyright © 1987, 1988, 1991 by Word Publishing, a division of Thomas Nelson, Inc. All rights reserved. Used by permission.

The New American Standard Bible®, (NASB) Copyright © 1960, 1962, 1963, 1968, 1971, 1972, 1973, 1975, 1977, 1995 by The Lockman Foundation. Used by permission.

The Holman Christian Standard Bible™ (HCSB) Copyright © 1999, 2000, 2001 by Holman Bible Publishers. Used by permission.

Cover Design by Kim Russell / Wahoo Designs
Page Layout by Bart Dawson

ISBN 978-1-60587-323-7

*Choose for yourselves this day
whom you will serve . . . .
But as for me and my house,
we will serve the Lord.*

—

Joshua 24:15 NKJV

100 Daily Prayers

For My Family

Introduction

Choose for yourselves this day whom you will serve . . . .
But as for me and my house, we will serve the Lord.
Joshua 24:15 NKJV

Your family is a priceless gift from God. What will you do with that gift? Will you pray for your loved ones? Will you do your best to create a loving home that honors the Creator and His only begotten Son? And will you treat all your family members with mutual respect, constant courtesy, patience, understanding, and forgiveness? Of course you should, and with God's help you can.

This book contains 100 devotional readings for moms and dads. Each chapter contains an essay, Bible verses, quotations, and a prayer, all of which can help you and your beloved focus on the blessings and opportunities that God has placed before you. The ideas on these pages are common-sense tools which can help you build your family's collective life upon the only foundation that can never be shaken—the foundation of God's Holy Word. God's promises are found in a book like no other: the Holy Bible. And as a Christian parent, you understand the need to trust God's promises, to follow His commandments, and to share the Good News of His Son.

As you face the inevitable challenges of modern-day family life—the ups, the downs, and the complications of life here in the 21st century—you should arm yourself with the promises and principles found in God's Word. When you do, then you and your loved ones can expect the best, not only for the day ahead but also for all eternity.

The Power of
Your Family's Prayers

If my people who are called by my name, will humble themselves and pray and seek my face and turn from their wicked ways, then will I hear from heaven and will forgive their sin and will heal their land.

2 Chronicles 7:14 NIV

Does your family pray together often, or just at church? Are you a little band of prayer warriors, or have you retreated from God's battlefield? Do you and yours pray only at mealtimes, or do you pray much more often than that? The answer to these questions will determine, to a surprising extent, the level of your family's spiritual health.

Jesus made it clear to His disciples: they should pray always. And so should you. Genuine, heartfelt prayer changes things and it changes you. When you lift your heart to the Father, you open yourself to a never-ending source of divine wisdom and infinite love.

Your family's prayers are powerful. So, as you go about your daily activities, remember God's instructions: "Rejoice always! Pray constantly. Give thanks in everything, for this is God's will for you in Christ Jesus" (1 Thessalonians 5:16-18 HCSB). Start praying in the morning and keep praying until you fall off to sleep at night. And rest assured: God is always listening, and He always wants to hear from you and your family.

Prayer connects us with
God's limitless potential.

—

Henry Blackaby

God shapes the world by prayer. The more praying there is in the world, the better the world will be, and the mightier will be the forces against evil.

E. M. Bounds

When there is a matter that requires definite prayer, pray until you believe God and until you can thank Him for His answer.

Hannah Whitall Smith

As we join together in prayer, we draw on God's enabling might in a way that multiplies our own efforts many times over.

Shirley Dobson

The intense prayer of the righteous is very powerful.

James 5:16 HCSB

Today's Prayer

Dear Lord, I will open my heart to You. I will take my concerns, my fears, my plans, and my hopes to You in prayer. And, then, I will trust the answers that You give. You are my loving Father, and I will accept Your will for my life today and every day that I live. Amen

Who's First?

Do not worship any other gods besides me.
Exodus 20:3 NLT

A s you and your family members think about the nature of your relationship with God, remember this: you will always have some type of relationship with Him—it is inevitable that your life must be lived in relationship to God. The question is not if you will have a relationship with Him; the burning question is whether or not that relationship will be one that seeks to honor Him . . . or not.

Are you willing to place God first in your life? And, are you willing to welcome God's Son into your heart? Unless you can honestly answer these questions with a resounding yes, then your relationship with God isn't what it could be or should be. Thankfully, God is always available, He's always ready to forgive, and He's waiting to hear from you now. The rest, of course, is up to you.

God is able to do anything He pleases with one ordinary person fully consecrated to Him.

Henry Blackaby and Claude King

When all else is gone, God is still left. Nothing changes Him.

Hannah Whitall Smith

God calls us to be committed to Him, to be committed to making a difference, and to be committed to reconciliation.

Bill Hybels

The thing you should want most is God's kingdom and doing what God wants. Then all these other things you need will be given to you.

Matthew 6:33 NCV

Today's Prayer

Dear Lord, today I will honor You with my thoughts, my actions, and my prayers. I will seek to please You, and I will strive to serve You. Your blessings are as limitless as Your love. And because I have been so richly blessed, I will worship You, Father, with thanksgiving in my heart and praise on my lips, this day and forever. Amen

You and Your Family

Unless the Lord builds a house,
its builders labor over it in vain; unless the Lord watches
over a city, the watchman stays alert in vain.

Psalm 127:1 HCSB

As every parent knows, family life is a mixture of conversations, mediations, irritations, deliberations, commiserations, frustrations, negotiations, and celebrations. In other words, the life of the typical parent is incredibly varied.

Certainly, in the life of every family, there are moments of frustration and disappointment. Lots of them. But, for those who are lucky enough to live in the presence of a close-knit, caring clan, the rewards far outweigh the frustrations.

No family is perfect, and neither is yours. But, despite the inevitable challenges and occasional hurt feelings of family life, your clan is God's gift to you. That little band of men, women, kids, and babies is a priceless treasure on temporary loan from the Father above. Give thanks to the Giver for the gift of family . . . and act accordingly.

There is so much compassion and understanding that is gained when we've experienced God's grace firsthand within our own families.

Lisa Whelchel

For whatever life holds for you and your family in the coming days, weave the unfailing fabric of God's Word through your heart and mind. It will hold strong, even if the rest of life unravels.

Gigi Graham Tchividjian

Never give your family the leftovers and crumbs of your time.

Charles Swindoll

Now these three remain: faith, hope, and love. But the greatest of these is love.

1 Corinthians 13:13 HCSB

Today's Prayer

Lord, You have given me a family to love and to care for. Thank You, Father. I will love all the members of my family despite their imperfections. Let them love me, Dear Lord, despite mine. Amen

Beyond Negativity

Don't speak evil against each other, my dear brothers and sisters. If you criticize each other and condemn each other, then you are criticizing and condemning God's law. But you are not a judge who can decide whether the law is right or wrong. Your job is to obey it.

James 4:11 NLT

From experience, we know that it is easier to criticize than to correct; we understand that it is easier to find faults than solutions; and we realize that excessive criticism is usually destructive, not productive. Yet the urge to criticize others remains a powerful temptation for most of us. Our task, as obedient believers, is to break the twin habits of negative thinking and critical speech.

Negativity is highly contagious: we give it to others who, in turn, give it back to us. This cycle can be broken by positive thoughts, heartfelt prayers, and encouraging words. As thoughtful servants of a loving God, we can use the transforming power of Christ's love to break the chains of negativity. And we should.

Winners see an answer for every problem; losers see a problem in every answer.

Barbara Johnson

Judging draws the judgment of others.

Catherine Marshall

Being critical of others, including God, is one way we try to avoid facing and judging our own sins.

Warren Wiersbe

After one hour in heaven, we shall be ashamed that we ever grumbled.

Vance Havner

Don't pick on people, jump on their failures, criticize their faults—unless, of course, you want the same treatment. Don't condemn those who are down; that hardness can boomerang. Be easy on people; you'll find life a lot easier.

Luke 6:37 MSG

Today's Prayer

Help me, Lord, rise above the need to criticize others. May my own shortcomings humble me, and may I always be a source of genuine encouragement to my family and friends. Amen

Follow Him

*"Follow Me," Jesus told them, "and I will make you
into fishers of men!" Immediately they left their nets
and followed Him.*
Mark 1:17-18 HCSB

Whom will you walk with today? Will you walk
with people who worship the ways of the
world? Or will you walk with the Son of God?
Jesus walks with you. Are you walking with Him?
Hopefully, you will choose to walk with Him today and
every day of your life.

Jesus has called upon believers of every generation
(and that includes you) to follow in His footsteps. And
God's Word promises that when you follow in Christ's
footsteps, you will learn how to live freely and lightly
(Matthew 11:28-30).

Are you worried about the day ahead? Be confident in
God's power. He will never desert you. Are you concerned
about the future? Be courageous and call upon God. He will
protect you. Are you confused? Listen to the quiet voice of
your Heavenly Father. He is not a God of confusion. Talk
with God; listen to Him; follow His commandments . . .
and walk with His Son—starting now.

Christ is like a river that is continually flowing.
There are always fresh supplies of water
coming from the fountain-head,
so that a man may live by it and
be supplied with water all his life.
So Christ is an ever-flowing fountain;
he is continually supplying his people,
and the fountain is not spent.
They who live upon Christ may have
fresh supplies from him for all eternity;
they may have an increase of blessedness
that is new, and new still,
and which never will come to an end.

—

Jonathan Edwards

Imagine the spiritual strength the disciples drew from walking hundreds of miles with Jesus . . . 3 John 4.

John Maxwell

Our responsibility is to feed from Him, to stay close to Him, to follow Him—because sheep easily go astray—so that we eternally experience the protection and companionship of our Great Shepherd the Lord Jesus Christ.

Franklin Graham

Jesus challenges you and me to keep our focus daily on the cross of His will if we want to be His disciples.

Anne Graham Lotz

Whoever serves me must follow me. Then my servant will be with me everywhere I am. My Father will honor anyone who serves me.

John 12:26 NCV

Today's Prayer

Dear Lord, You sent Jesus to save the world and to save me. I thank You for Jesus, and I will do my best to follow Him, today and forever. Amen

Forgiveness Now

Then Peter came to him and asked, "Lord, how often should
I forgive someone who sins against me? Seven times?"
"No!" Jesus replied, "seventy times seven!"
Matthew 18:21-22 NLT

Even the most mild-mannered parents will, on occasion, have reason to become angry with the shortcomings of family members and friends. But wise moms and dads are quick to forgive others, just as God has forgiven them.

Forgiveness is God's commandment, but oh how difficult a commandment it can be to follow. Being frail, fallible, imperfect human beings, we are quick to anger, quick to blame, slow to forgive, and even slower to forget. No matter. Forgiveness, no matter how difficult, is God's way, and it must be our way, too.

If, in your heart, you hold bitterness against even a single person, forgive. If there exists even one person, alive or dead, whom you have not forgiven, follow God's commandment and His will for your life: forgive. If you are embittered against yourself for some past mistake or shortcoming, forgive. Then, to the best of your abilities, forget. And move on. Hatred, bitterness, and regret are not part of God's plan for your life. Forgiveness is.

There is always room
for more loving forgiveness
within our homes.

—

James Dobson

Learning how to forgive and forget is one of the secrets of a happy Christian life.

Warren Wiersbe

God's heart of mercy provides for us not only pardon from sin but also a daily provision of spiritual food to strengthen us.

Jim Cymbala

God expects us to forgive others as He has forgiven us; we are to follow His example by having a forgiving heart.

Vonette Bright

Be gentle with one another, sensitive. Forgive one another as quickly and thoroughly as God in Christ forgave you.

Ephesians 4:32 MSG

Today's Prayer

Lord, I know that I need to forgive others just as You have forgiven me. Help me to be an example of forgiveness to my children. Keep me mindful, Father, that I am never fully liberated until I have been freed from the chains of bitterness—and that You offer me that freedom through Your Son, Christ Jesus. Amen

Time for Fun

*So I recommend having fun, because there is nothing better
for people to do in this world than to eat, drink, and enjoy life.
That way they will experience some happiness along
with all the hard work God gives them.*
Ecclesiastes 8:15 NLT

Are you a parent who takes time each day to really enjoy your family and your life? Hopefully so. After all, you are the recipient of a precious gift—the gift of life. And because God has seen fit to give you this gift, it is incumbent upon you to use it and to enjoy it. But sometimes, amid the inevitable pressures of everyday living, really enjoying life may seem almost impossible. It is not.

For most of us, fun is as much a function of attitude as it is a function of environment. So whether you're standing victorious atop one of life's mountains or trudging through one of life's valleys, enjoy yourself. You deserve to have fun today, and God wants you to have fun today . . . so what on earth are you waiting for?

If we don't hunger and thirst after righteousness, we'll become anemic and feel miserable in our Christian experience.

Franklin Graham

True happiness and contentment cannot come from the things of this world. The blessedness of true joy is a free gift that comes only from our Lord and Savior, Jesus Christ.

Dennis Swanberg

The happiest people in the world are not those who have no problems, but the people who have learned to live with those things that are less than perfect.

James Dobson

Rejoice in the Lord always. I will say it again: Rejoice!

Philippians 4:4 HCSB

Today's Prayer

Dear Lord, You are my strength and my joy. I will rejoice in the day that You have made, and I will give thanks for the countless blessings that You have given me. Let me be a joyful Christian, Father, as I share the Good News of Your Son, and let me praise You for all the marvelous things you have done. Amen

Your Bright Future

What a God we have! And how fortunate we are to have him, this Father of our Master Jesus! Because Jesus was raised from the dead, we've been given a brand-new life and have everything to live for, including a future in heaven—and the future starts now!

1 Peter 1:3-4 MSG

How bright is your future? Well, if you're a faithful believer, God's plans for you are so bright that you'd better wear shades. But here's an important question: How bright do you believe your future to be? Are you expecting a terrific tomorrow, or are you dreading a terrible one? The answer you give will have a powerful impact on the way tomorrow turns out.

Do you trust in the ultimate goodness of God's plan for your life? Will you face tomorrow's challenges with optimism and hope? You should. After all, God created you for a very important reason: His reason. And you still have important work to do: His work.

Today, as you live in the present and look to the future, remember that God has an amazing plan for you. Act—and believe—accordingly.

Do not limit the limitless God! With Him, face the future unafraid because you are never alone.

Mrs. Charles E. Cowman

Hoping for a good future without investing in today is like a farmer waiting for a crop without ever planting any seed.

John Maxwell

The pages of your past cannot be rewritten, but the pages of your tomorrows are blank.

Zig Ziglar

The Christian believes in a fabulous future.

Billy Graham

Wisdom is pleasing to you. If you find it, you have hope for the future.

Proverbs 24:14 NCV

Today's Prayer

Dear Lord, as I look to the future, I will place my trust in You. If I become discouraged, I will turn to You. If I am afraid, I will seek strength in You. You are my Father, and I will place my hope, my trust, and my faith in You. Amen

The Wisdom
to Be Generous

The good person is generous and lends lavishly . . . .
Psalm 112:5 MSG

God's gifts are beyond description, His blessings beyond comprehension. God has been incredibly generous with us, and He rightfully expects us to be generous with others. That's why the thread of generosity is woven into the very fabric of God's teachings.

In the Old Testament, we are told that, "The good person is generous and lends lavishly . . . ." (Psalm 112:5 MSG). And in the New Testament we are instructed, "Freely you have received, freely give" (Matthew 10:8 NKJV). These principles still apply. As we establish priorities for our days and our lives, we are advised to give freely of our time, our possessions, and our love—just as God has given freely to us.

Of course, we can never fully repay God for His gifts, but we can share them with others. And we should.

Nothing is really ours until we share it.

C. S. Lewis

We are never more like God than when we give.

Charles Swindoll

If you want to be truly happy, you won't find it on an endless quest for more stuff. You'll find it in receiving God's generosity and then passing that generosity along.

Bill Hybels

The measure of a life, after all, is not its duration but its donation.

Corrie ten Boom

Freely you have received, freely give.

Matthew 10:8 NIV

Today's Prayer

Dear Lord, You have been so generous with me; let me be generous with others. Help me to be generous with my time and my possessions as I care for those in need. Help me to teach my children to be cheerful givers, Father, and make us all humble givers, so that the glory and the praise might be Yours. Amen

Using God's Gifts

Each one has his own gift from God,
one in this manner and another in that.
1 Corinthians 7:7 NKJV

Your talents are a gift from God. And, the same applies to your children. Their talents, too, are blessings from the Creator, blessings which must be nurtured or forfeited.

Are you and your loved ones willing to use your gifts in the way that God intends? Are you willing to summon the discipline that is required to develop your talents and to hone your skills? That's precisely what God wants you to do, and that's precisely what you should desire for yourselves.

So be faithful stewards of your talents and treasures. And then prepare yourselves for even greater blessings that are sure to come.

Not everyone possesses boundless energy or a conspicuous talent. We are not equally blessed with great intellect or physical beauty or emotional strength. But we have all been given the same ability to be faithful.

Gigi Graham Tchividjian

If you want to reach your potential, you need to add a strong work ethic to your talent.

John Maxwell

You are the only person on earth who can use your ability.

Zig Ziglar

This is why I remind you to keep using the gift God gave you when I laid my hands on you. Now let it grow, as a small flame grows into a fire.

2 Timothy 1:6 NCV

Today's Prayer

Dear Lord, let me use my gifts, and let me help my children discover theirs. Your gifts are priceless and eternal—may we, as Your faithful children, use our own gifts to the glory of Your kingdom, today and forever. Amen

God Can Handle It

For I, the Lord your God,
hold your right hand and say to you:
Do not fear, I will help you.
Isaiah 41:13 HCSB

It's a promise that is made over and over again in the Bible: Whatever "it" is, God can handle it.

Life isn't always easy. Far from it! Sometimes, life can be very, very tough. But even then, even during our darkest moments, we're protected by a loving Heavenly Father. When we're worried, God can reassure us; when we're sad, God can comfort us. When our families are hurting, God is not just near; He is here. So we must lift our thoughts and prayers to Him. When we do, He will answer our prayers. Why? Because He is our shepherd, and He has promised to protect us now and forever.

Fill your mind with thoughts of God rather than thoughts of fear.

Norman Vincent Peale

God uses our most stumbling, faltering faith-steps as the open door to His doing for us "more than we ask or think."

Catherine Marshall

God is always sufficient in perfect proportion to our need.

Beth Moore

God's saints in all ages have realized that God was enough for them. God is enough for time; God is enough for eternity. God is enough!

Hannah Whitall Smith

Be of good courage, and He shall strengthen your heart, all you who hope in the Lord.

Psalm 31:24 NKJV

Today's Prayer

Dear Lord, whatever "it" is, You can handle it! Let me turn to You when I am fearful or worried. You are my loving Heavenly Father, sufficient in all things and I will always trust You. Amen

Tackling Tough Times

God is our refuge and strength,
always ready to help in times of trouble.
So we will not fear, even if earthquakes come
and mountains crumble to the sea.

Psalm 46:1-2 NLT

From time to time, all of us face adversity, hardship, disappointment, and loss. Old Man Trouble pays periodic visits to each of us; none of our families are exempt. When we are troubled, God stands ready and willing to protect us. Our responsibility, of course, is to ask Him for protection. When we call upon Him in heartfelt prayer, He will answer—in His own time and in accordance with His own perfect plan.

Our world continues to change, but God's love remains constant. He remains ready to comfort us and strengthen us whenever we turn to Him. Psalm 145 promises, "The Lord is near to all who call on him, to all who call on him in truth. He fulfills the desires of those who fear him; he hears their cry and saves them" (vv. 18-20 NIV).

Life is often challenging, but as Christians, we must not be afraid. God loves us, and He will protect us. In times of hardship, He will comfort us; in times of sorrow, He will dry our tears. When we are troubled, weak, or sorrowful, God is always with us and our families. We must build our lives on the rock that cannot be shaken . . . we must trust in God always. And we must encourage our loved ones to do the same.

> Your greatest ministry
> will likely come out of
> your greatest hurt.
>
> —
>
> Rick Warren

God will not permit any troubles to come upon us unless He has a specific plan by which great blessing can come out of the difficulty.

Peter Marshall

Jesus does not say, "There is no storm." He says, "I am here, do not toss, but trust."

Vance Havner

The strengthening of faith comes from staying with it in the hour of trial. We should not shrink from tests of faith.

Catherine Marshall

We are hard pressed on every side, yet not crushed; we are perplexed, but not in despair.

2 Corinthians 4:8 NKJV

Today's Prayer

Heavenly Father, You are my strength and my refuge. As I journey through this day, I know that I may encounter disappointments and losses. When I am troubled, let me turn to You. Keep me steady, Lord, and renew a right spirit inside of me this day and forever. Amen

God Is Love

*God is love, and the one who remains in love
remains in God,
and God remains in him.*
1 John 4:16 HCSB

The Bible makes this promise: God is love. It's a sweeping statement, a profoundly important description of what God is and how God works. God's love is perfect. When we open our hearts to His perfect love, we are touched by the Creator's hand, and we are transformed.

Today, even if you can only carve out a few quiet moments, offer sincere prayers of thanksgiving to your Creator. Thank Him for His blessings and His love. As you sit in silence, open your heart to the Father, and do your best to sense His presence. When you do, you'll discover the genuine peace that only the Creator can provide. That peace, of course, flows from the loving heart of God. You can experience His peace and His love today . . . and you should.

Let God have you,
and let God love you—
and don't be surprised
if your heart begins to hear music
you've never heard
and your feet learn to dance
as never before.

—

Max Lucado

I can tell you, from personal experience of walking with God for over fifty years, that He is the Lover of my soul.

Vonette Bright

God loves these people too, just because they're unattractive or warped in their thinking doesn't mean the Lord doesn't love them.

Ruth Bell Graham

Even when we cannot see the why and wherefore of God's dealings, we know that there is love in and behind them, so we can rejoice always.

J. I. Packer

For the Lord is good, and His love is eternal; His faithfulness endures through all generations.

Psalm 100:5 HCSB

Today's Prayer

Dear Lord, the Bible tells me that You are my loving Father. I thank You, Lord, for Your love and for Your Son. Amen

---

Celebrate!

Celebrate God all day, every day. I mean, revel in him!
Philippians 4:4 MSG

Are you a parent who celebrates life? Hopefully you are! God has richly blessed you, and He wants you to rejoice in His gifts.

God fills each day to the brim with possibilities, and He challenges each of us to use our gifts for the glory of His kingdom. When we honor the Father and place Him at the center of our lives, every day becomes a cause for celebration.

Today is a non-renewable resource—once it's gone, it's gone forever. Our responsibility—both as parents and as believers—is to use this day in the service of God's will and in the service of His people. When we do so, we enrich our own lives and the lives of those whom we love. And the Father smiles.

If you can forgive the person you were, accept the person you are, and believe in the person you will become, you are headed for joy. So celebrate your life.

Barbara Johnson

Our sense of joy, satisfaction, and fulfillment in life increases, no matter what the circumstances, if we are in the center of God's will.

Billy Graham

This is the day the LORD has made; we will rejoice and be glad in it.

Psalm 118:24 NKJV

Today's Prayer

Dear Lord, You have given me so many reasons to celebrate. Today, let me choose an attitude of cheerfulness. Let me be a joyful Christian, Lord, quick to laugh and slow to anger. Let me praise You, Lord, and give thanks for Your blessings. Today is Your creation; let me celebrate it . . . and You. Amen

Your Children: A Treasure from God

*Train up a child in the way he should go,
and when he is old he will not depart from it.*

Proverbs 22:6 NKJV

As a parent, you are keenly aware that God has entrusted you with a priceless treasure from above: your child. Every child is different, yet every child is similar in this respect: every child is a glorious gift from above—and with that gift comes immense responsibilities.

Thoughtful parents (like you) understand the critical importance of raising their children with love, with family, with discipline, and with God. By making God a focus in the home, loving parents offer a priceless legacy to their children—a legacy of hope, a legacy of love, a legacy of wisdom.

Today, let us pray for our children . . . all of them. Let us pray for our own children and for children around the world. Every child is God's child. May we, as concerned parents, behave—and pray—accordingly.

Our faithfulness, or lack of it,
will have an overwhelming impact
on the heritage of our children.

—

Beth Moore

He intended families to be the safe haven where children are born and raised, a place where the tender shoots are nurtured until their roots grow strong and deep.

Carol Kuykendall

Happy is the child who happens in upon his parent from time to time to see him on his knees, or going aside regularly, to keep times with the Lord.

Larry Christenson

When Jesus realized how much this mattered to them, he brought a child to his side. "Whoever accepts this child as if the child were me, accepts me," he said. "And whoever accepts me, accepts the One who sent me. You become great by accepting, not asserting. Your spirit, not your size, makes the difference."

Luke 9:47-48 MSG

Today's Prayer

Lord, You have given me a wonderful responsibility: caring for my children. Let me love them, care for them, nurture them, teach them, and lead them to You. When I am weary, give me strength. When I am frustrated, give me patience. And, let my words and deeds always demonstrate to my children the love that I feel for them . . . and for You. Amen

Studying the Word

All Scripture is inspired by God and is profitable for teaching,
for rebuking, for correcting, for training in righteousness,
so that the man of God may be complete,
equipped for every good work.
2 Timothy 3:16-17 HCSB

God's Word is unlike any other book. The Bible is a roadmap for life here on earth and for life eternal. As Christians, we are called upon to study God's Holy Word, to trust His Word, to follow its commandments, and to share its Good News with the world.

The words of Matthew 4:4 remind us that, "Man shall not live by bread alone but by every word that proceedeth out of the mouth of God" (KJV). As believers, we must study the Bible and meditate upon its meaning for our lives. Otherwise, we deprive ourselves of a priceless gift from our Creator.

Warren Wiersbe observed, "When the child of God looks into the Word of God, he sees the Son of God. And, he is transformed by the Spirit of God to share in the glory of God." God's Holy Word is, indeed, a transforming, life-changing, one-of-a-kind treasure. And, a passing acquaintance with the Good Book is insufficient for Christians who seek to obey God's Word and to understand His will. After all, man does not live by bread alone. And neither should families.

Study the Bible and observe
how the persons behaved
and how God dealt with them.
There is explicit teaching
on every condition of life.

—

Corrie ten Boom

The Reference Point for the Christian is the Bible. All values, judgments, and attitudes must be gauged in relationship to this Reference Point.

Ruth Bell Graham

Nobody ever outgrows Scripture; the book widens and deepens with our years.

C. H. Spurgeon

The Bible is a remarkable commentary on perspective. Through its divine message, we are brought face to face with issues and tests in daily living and how, by the power of the Holy Spirit, we are enabled to respond positively to them.

Luci Swindoll

For I am not ashamed of the gospel, because it is God's power for salvation to everyone who believes.

Romans 1:16 HCSB

Today's Prayer

Dear Lord, the Bible is Your gift to me. Let me use it, let me trust it, and let me obey it, today and every day that I live. Amen

Your Real Treasures

I will bless them and the places surrounding my hill.
I will send down showers in season;
there will be showers of blessings.
Ezekiel 34:26 NIV

B ecause you are a parent, you have been specially blessed by the Creator. God has given you blessings that are, in truth, simply too numerous to count. Your blessings include life, family, freedom, friends, talents, and possessions, for starters. But, your greatest blessing—a priceless treasure that is yours for the asking—is God's gift of salvation through Christ Jesus.

The gifts you receive from God are multiplied when you share them with others. Today, give thanks to God for your blessings and demonstrate your gratitude by sharing those blessings with your family, with your friends, and with the world.

Do we not continually pass by blessings innumerable without notice, and instead fix our eyes on what we feel to be our trials and our losses, and think and talk about these until our whole horizon is filled with them, and we almost begin to think we have no blessings at all?

Hannah Whitall Smith

Think of the blessings we so easily take for granted: Life itself; preservation from danger; every bit of health we enjoy; every hour of liberty; the ability to see, to hear, to speak, to think, and to imagine all this comes from the hand of God.

Billy Graham

The Lord bless you and keep you; the Lord make His face shine upon you, and be gracious to you.

Numbers 6:24-25 NKJV

Today's Prayer

Lord, let me be a parent who is quick to count Your blessings. And let me be Your faithful servant as I give praise to the Giver of all things good. You have richly blessed my life, Lord. Let me, in turn, be a blessing to my family and my world—and may the glory be Yours forever. Amen

Too Busy?

Come to Me, all you who are weary and burdened,
and I will give you rest. Take My yoke upon you
and learn from Me, because I am gentle and humble in heart,
and you will find rest for your souls.
For My yoke is easy and My burden is light.
Matthew 11:28-30 HCSB

If you're a parent with too many responsibilities and too few hours in which to fulfill them, you are not alone. The job of parenting can be so demanding that sometimes you may feel as if you have no time for yourself . . . and no time for God.

Has the busy pace of life robbed you of the peace that might otherwise be yours through Jesus Christ? If so, you are simply too busy for your own good. Through His Son Jesus, God offers you a peace that passes human understanding, but He won't force His peace upon you; in order to experience it, you must slow down long enough to sense His presence and His love.

Today, as a gift to yourself, to your family, and to the world, slow down long enough to claim the inner peace that is your spiritual birthright: the peace of Jesus Christ.

It is offered freely; it has been paid for in full; it is yours for the asking. So ask. And then share.

Frustration is not the will of God. There is time to do anything and everything that God wants us to do.

—

Elisabeth Elliot

Being busy, in and of itself, is not a sin. But being busy in an endless pursuit of things that leave us empty and hollow and broken inside—that cannot be pleasing to God.

Max Lucado

In our tense, uptight society where folks are rushing to make appointments they have already missed, a good laugh can be as refreshing as a cup of cold water in the desert.

Barbara Johnson

Don't burn out; keep yourselves fueled and aflame. Be alert servants of the Master, cheerfully expectant. Don't quit in hard times; pray all the harder.

Romans 12:11-12 MSG

Today's Prayer

Dear Lord, sometimes, I am distracted by the busyness of the day or the demands of the moment. When I am worried or anxious, Father, turn my thoughts back to You. Help me to trust Your will, to follow Your commands, and to accept Your peace, today and forever. Amen

The Right Kind of Attitude

*And now, dear brothers and sisters, let me say one more thing
as I close this letter. Fix your thoughts on what is true
and honorable and right. Think about things that are pure
and lovely and admirable. Think about things
that are excellent and worthy of praise.*

Philippians 4:8 NLT

The Christian life is a cause for celebration, but sometimes we don't feel much like celebrating. In fact, when the weight of the world seems to bear down upon our shoulders, celebration may be the last thing on our minds . . . but it shouldn't be. As God's children—and as the parents of our own children—we are all blessed beyond measure on good days and bad. This day is a non-renewable resource: once it's gone, it's gone forever. We should give thanks for this day while using it for the glory of God.

What will be your attitude today? Will you be fearful, angry, bored, or worried? Will you be cynical, bitter, or pessimistic? If so, God wants to have a little talk with you.

God created you in His own image, and He wants you to experience joy and abundance. But, God will not force His joy upon you; you must claim it for yourself. So today, and every day hereafter, celebrate the life that God has given you. Think optimistically about yourself and your future. Give thanks to the One who has given you everything, and trust in your heart that He wants to give you so much more.

Keep your feet on the ground, but let your heart soar as high as it will. Refuse to be average or to surrender to the chill of your spiritual environment.

—

A. W. Tozer

The people whom I have seen succeed best in life have always been cheerful and hopeful people who went about their business with a smile on their faces.

Charles Kingsley

The essence of optimism is that it takes no account of the present, but it is a source of inspiration, of vitality, and of hope. Where others have resigned, it enables a man to hold his head high, to claim the future for himself, and not abandon it to his enemy.

Dietrich Bonhoeffer

Set your minds on what is above, not on what is on the earth.

Colossians 3:2 HCSB

Today's Prayer

Lord, let me be an expectant Christian. Let me expect the best from You, and let me look for the best in others. If I become discouraged, Father, turn my thoughts and my prayers to You. Let me trust You, Lord, to direct my life. And, let me share my faith and optimism with others, today and every day that I live. Amen

---

Your Beliefs

Do what God's teaching says;
when you only listen and do nothing,
you are fooling yourselves.
James 1:22 NCV

In describing one's beliefs, actions are far better descriptors than words. Yet far too many of us spend more energy talking about our beliefs than living by them—with predictable consequences.

Is your life a picture book of your creed? Are your actions congruent with your beliefs? Are you willing to practice the philosophy that you preach?

Today and every day, make certain that your actions are guided by God's Word and by the conscience that He has placed in your heart. Don't treat your faith as if it were separate from your everyday life. Weave your beliefs into the very fabric of your day. When you do, God will honor your good works, and your good works will honor God.

Once you have thoroughly examined your values and articulated them, you will be able to steer your life by them.

John Maxwell

Believe and do what God says. The life-changing consequences will be limitless, and the results will be confidence and peace of mind.

Franklin Graham

God calls us to be committed to Him, to be committed to making a difference, and to be committed to reconciliation.

Bill Hybels

Let not your heart be troubled: ye believe in God, believe also in me.

John 14:1 KJV

Today's Prayer

Heavenly Father, I believe in You, and I believe in Your Word. Help me to live in such a way that my actions validate my beliefs—and let the glory be Yours forever. Amen

Courage for Difficult Days

Be strong and courageous, and do the work. Do not be afraid or discouraged, for the Lord God, my God, is with you.
1 Chronicles 28:20 NIV

Being a godly parent in this difficult world is no easy task. Ours is a time of uncertainty and danger, a time when even the most courageous moms and dads have legitimate cause for concern. But as believers we can live courageously, knowing that we have been saved by a loving Father and His only begotten Son.

Are you anxious? Take those anxieties to God. Are you troubled? Take your troubles to Him. Does the world seem to be trembling beneath your feet? Seek protection from the One who cannot be moved. The same God who created the universe will protect you if you ask Him . . . so ask Him. And then live courageously, knowing that even in these troubled times, God is always as near as your next breath.

Take courage. We walk in the wilderness today and in the Promised Land tomorrow.

D. L. Moody

Do not let Satan deceive you into being afraid of God's plans for your life.

R. A. Torrey

The fear of God is the death of every other fear.

C. H. Spurgeon

When once we are assured that God is good, then there can be nothing left to fear.

Hannah Whitall Smith

The Lord is the One who will go before you. He will be with you; He will not leave you or forsake you. Do not be afraid or discouraged.

Deuteronomy 31:8 HCSB

Today's Prayer

Lord, at times, this world is a fearful place. I fear for my family and especially for my children. Yet, You have promised me that You are with me always. With You as my protector, I am not afraid. Today, Dear Lord, let me live courageously as I place my trust in You. Amen

---

God's Good News

Thanks be to God for his indescribable gift!
2 Corinthians 9:15 NIV

Christ died on the cross so that we might have eternal life. This gift, freely given from God's only Son, is the priceless possession of everyone who accepts Him as Lord and Savior.

Thankfully, God's grace is not an earthly reward for righteous behavior; it is, instead, a blessed spiritual gift. When we accept Christ into our hearts, we are saved by His grace. The familiar words from the book of Ephesians make God's promise perfectly clear: "For it is by grace you have been saved, through faith—and this not from yourselves, it is the gift of God—not by works, so that no one can boast" (2:8-9 NIV).

God's grace is the ultimate gift, and we owe Him our eternal gratitude. Our Heavenly Father is waiting patiently for each of us to accept His Son and receive His grace. Let us accept that gift today so that we might enjoy God's presence now and throughout all eternity.

No one is beyond his grace. No situation, anywhere on earth, is too hard for God.

Jim Cymbala

God does amazing works through prayers that seek to extend His grace to others.

Shirley Dobson

In your greatest weakness, turn to your greatest strength, Jesus, and hear Him say, "My grace is sufficient for you, for My strength is made perfect in weakness" (2 Corinthians 12:9, NKJV).

Lisa Whelchel

So we're not giving up. How could we! Even though on the outside it often looks like things are falling apart on us, on the inside, where God is making new life, not a day goes by without his unfolding grace.

2 Corinthians 4:16 MSG

Today's Prayer

Accepting Your grace can be hard, Lord. Somehow, I feel that I must earn Your love and Your acceptance. Yet, the Bible promises that You love me and save me by Your grace. It is a gift I can only accept and cannot earn. Thank You for Your priceless, everlasting gift. Amen

God's Guidance

Every morning he wakes me. He teaches me to listen
like a student. The Lord God helps me learn . . .
Isaiah 50:4-5 NCV

The Bible promises that God will guide you if you let Him. Your job, of course, is to let Him. But sometimes, you will be tempted to do otherwise. Sometimes, you'll be tempted to go along with the crowd; other times, you'll be tempted to do things your way, not God's way. When you feel those temptations, resist them.

What will you allow to guide you through the coming day: your own desires (or, for that matter, the desires of your friends)? Or will you allow God to lead the way? The answer should be obvious. You should let God be your guide. When you entrust your life to Him completely and without reservation, God will give you the strength to meet any challenge, the courage to face any trial, and the wisdom to live in His righteousness. So trust Him today and seek His guidance. When you do, your next step will be the right one.

Fix your eyes upon the Lord! Do it once. Do it daily. Do it constantly. Look at the Lord and keep looking at Him.

Charles Swindoll

We must always invite Jesus to be the navigator of our plans, desires, wills, and emotions, for He is the way, the truth, and the life.

Bill Bright

It is a joy that God never abandons His children. He guides faithfully all who listen to His directions.

Corrie ten Boom

The LORD says, "I will guide you along the best pathway for your life. I will advise you and watch over you."

Psalm 32:8 NLT

Today's Prayer

Dear Lord, thank You for Your constant presence and Your constant love. I draw near to You this day with the confidence that You are ready to guide me. Help me walk closely with You, Father, and help me share Your Good News with all who cross my path. Amen

Every Day with God

*Morning by morning he wakens me and opens
my understanding to his will.
The Sovereign Lord has spoken to me, and I have listened.*
Isaiah 50:4-5 NLT

Each new day is a gift from God, and wise parents spend a few quiet moments each morning thanking the Giver. Daily life is woven together with the threads of habit, and no habit is more important to our spiritual health than the discipline of daily prayer and devotion to the Creator.

When we begin each day with heads bowed and hearts lifted, we remind ourselves of God's love, His protection, and His commandments. And if we are wise, we align our priorities for the coming day with the teachings and commandments that God has given us through His Holy Word.

Are you seeking to change some aspect of your life? Then take time out of your hectic schedule to spend time each day with your Creator. Ask for God's help and ask for it many times each day . . . starting with your morning devotional.

I suggest you discipline yourself to spend time daily in a systematic reading of God's Word. Make this "quiet time" a priority that nobody can change.

Warren Wiersbe

If you, too, will learn to wait upon God, to get alone with Him, and remain silent so that you can hear His voice when He is ready to speak to you, what a difference it will make in your life!

Kay Arthur

We must appropriate the tender mercy of God every day after conversion or problems quickly develop. We need His grace daily in order to live a righteous life.

Jim Cymbala

Stay clear of silly stories that get dressed up as religion. Exercise daily in God—no spiritual flabbiness, please!

1 Timothy 4:7 MSG

Today's Prayer

Lord, help me to hear Your direction for my life in the quiet moments when I study Your Holy Word. And as I go about my daily activities, let everything that I say and do be pleasing to You. Amen

Too Many Distractions?

Let us lay aside every weight and the sin
that so easily ensnares us, and run with endurance
the race that lies before us, keeping our eyes on Jesus,
the source and perfecter of our faith.

Hebrews 12:1-2 HCSB

All of us must live through those days when the traffic jams, the computer crashes, and the dog makes a main course out of our homework. But, when we find ourselves distracted by the minor frustrations of life, we must catch ourselves, take a deep breath, and lift our thoughts upward.

Although we may, at times, struggle mightily to rise above the distractions of the everyday living, we need never struggle alone. God is here—eternal and faithful, with infinite patience and love—and, if we reach out to Him, He will restore our sense of perspective and give peace to our souls.

There is an enormous power in little things to distract our attention from God.

Oswald Chambers

Setting goals is one way you can be sure that you will focus your efforts on the main things so that trivial matters will not become your focus.

Charles Stanley

When Jesus is in our midst, He brings His limitless power along as well. But, Jesus must be in the middle, all eyes and hearts focused on Him.

Shirley Dobson

We need to stop focusing on our lacks and stop giving out excuses and start looking at and listening to Jesus.

Anne Graham Lotz

Do not worship any other gods besides me.

Exodus 20:3 NLT

Today's Prayer

Dear Lord, help me to face this day with a spirit of optimism and thanksgiving. And let me focus my thoughts on You and Your incomparable gifts. Amen

Big Dreams

With God's power working in us, God can do much,
much more than anything we can ask or imagine.

Ephesians 3:20 NCV

Are you willing to entertain the possibility that God has big plans in store for you? Hopefully so. Yet sometimes, especially if you've recently experienced a life-altering disappointment, you may find it difficult to envision a brighter future for yourself and your family. If so, it's time to reconsider your own capabilities . . . and God's.

Your Heavenly Father created you with unique gifts and untapped talents; your job is to tap them. When you do, you'll begin to feel an increasing sense of confidence in yourself and in your future.

It takes courage to dream big dreams. You will discover that courage when you do three things: accept the past, trust God to handle the future, and make the most of the time He has given you today.

Nothing is too difficult for God, and no dreams are too big for Him—not even yours. So start living—and dreaming—accordingly.

The future lies all before us. Shall it only be a slight advance upon what we usually do? Ought it not to be a bound, a leap forward to altitudes of endeavor and success undreamed of before?

Annie Armstrong

You cannot out-dream God.

John Eldredge

Set goals so big that unless God helps you, you will be a miserable failure.

Bill Bright

Now may the God of hope fill you with all joy and peace in believing, so that you may overflow with hope by the power of the Holy Spirit.

Romans 15:13 HCSB

Today's Prayer

Dear Lord, give me the courage to dream and the faithfulness to trust in Your perfect plan. When I am worried or weary, give me strength for today and hope for tomorrow. Keep me mindful of Your healing power, Your infinite love, and Your eternal salvation. Amen

The Gift of Encouragement

Let's see how inventive we can be in encouraging love
and helping out, not avoiding worshipping together
as some do but spurring each other on.
Hebrews 10:24-25 MSG

Every member of your family needs a regular supply of encouraging words and pats on the back. And you need the rewards that God gives to those enthusiastic parents who are a continual source of encouragement to their loved ones.

In his letter to the Ephesians, Paul writes, "Do not let any unwholesome talk come out of your mouths, but only what is helpful for building others up according to their needs, that it may benefit those who listen" (4:29 NIV). This passage reminds us that, as Christians, we are instructed to choose our words carefully so as to build others up through wholesome, honest encouragement. How can we build others up? By celebrating their victories and their accomplishments. As the old saying goes, "When someone does something good, applaud—you'll make two people happy."

Today, look for the good in others—starting with your family. And then, celebrate the good that you find. When you do, you'll be a powerful force of encouragement in the world . . . and a worthy servant to your God.

A lot of people have gone further than they thought they could because someone else thought they could.

Zig Ziglar

Words. Do you fully understand their power? Can any of us really grasp the mighty force behind the things we say? Do we stop and think before we speak, considering the potency of the words we utter?

Joni Eareckson Tada

Kind words are like honey—sweet to the soul and healthy for the body.

Proverbs 16:24 NLT

Today's Prayer

Dear Father, make me an encouraging parent. Just as You have lifted me up, let me also lift up my children in the spirit of encouragement and hope. Today, let me help my children find the strength and the courage to use their gifts according to Your master plan. Amen

Enthused About Life

*Whatever you do, do it enthusiastically,
as something done for the Lord and not for men.*
Colossians 3:23 HCSB

Do you see each day as a glorious opportunity to serve God and to do His will? Are you enthused about life, or do you struggle through each day giving scarcely a thought to God's blessings? Are you constantly praising God for His gifts, and are you sharing His Good News with your children? And are you excited about the possibilities for service that God has placed before you, whether at home, at work, or at church? You should be.

You are the recipient of Christ's sacrificial love. Accept it enthusiastically and share it fervently. Jesus deserves your enthusiasm; your family deserves it; the world deserves it; and you deserve the experience of sharing it.

Enthusiasm, like the flu, is contagious—we get it from one another.

Barbara Johnson

Wherever you are, be all there. Live to the hilt every situation you believe to be the will of God.

Jim Elliot

Catch on fire with enthusiasm and people will come for miles to watch you burn.

John Wesley

When we wholeheartedly commit ourselves to God, there is nothing mediocre or run-of-the-mill about us. To live for Christ is to be passionate about our Lord and about our lives.

Jim Gallery

Never be lazy in your work, but serve the Lord enthusiastically.

Romans 12:11 NLT

Today's Prayer

Dear Lord, You have called me not to a life of mediocrity, but to a life of passion. Today, I will be an enthusiastic follower of Your Son, and I will share His Good News—and His love—with all who cross my path. Amen

On Guard Against Evil

Your love must be real.
Hate what is evil, and hold on to what is good.
Romans 12:9 NCV

This world is God's creation, and it contains the wonderful fruits of His handiwork. But, it also contains countless opportunities to stray from God's will. Temptations are everywhere, and the devil, it seems, never takes a day off. Our task, as caring parents, is to do all that we can to protect our families from the evils of the world.

We must recognize evil and fight it. When we observe life objectively, and when we do so with eyes and hearts that are attuned to God's Holy Word, we can no longer be neutral believers. And when we are no longer neutral, God rejoices while the devil despairs.

Christianity isn't a religion about going to Sunday school, potluck suppers, being nice, holding car washes, sending your secondhand clothes off to Mexico—as good as those things might be. This is a world at war.

John Eldredge

God loves you, and He yearns for you to turn away from the path of evil. You need His forgiveness, and you need Him to come into your life and remake you from within.

Billy Graham

Where God's ministers are most successful, there the powers of darkness marshal their forces for the conflict.

Lottie Moon

The Lord is pleased with a good person, but he will punish anyone who plans evil.

Proverbs 12:2 NCV

Today's Prayer

Lord, strengthen my walk with You. Evil comes in many disguises, and sometimes it is only with Your help that I can recognize right from wrong. Your presence in my life enables me to choose truth and to live a life pleasing to You. May I always live in Your presence. Amen

What Kind of Example?

You should be an example to the believers in speech,
in conduct, in love, in faith, in purity.
1 Timothy 4:12 HCSB

Our children learn from the lessons we teach and the lives we live, but not necessarily in that order. What kind of example are you? Are you the kind of parent whose life serves as a genuine example of patience and righteousness? Are you a person whose behavior serves as a positive role model for others? Are you the kind of parent whose actions, day in and day out, are based upon kindness, faithfulness, and a sincere love for the Lord? If so, you are not only blessed by God, but you are also a powerful force for good in a world that desperately needs positive influences such as yours.

Corrie ten Boom advised, "Don't worry about what you do not understand. Worry about what you do understand in the Bible but do not live by." And that's sound advice because our families and friends are watching . . . and so, for that matter, is God.

In your desire to share the gospel, you may be the only Jesus someone else will ever meet. Be real and be involved with people.

Barbara Johnson

Among the most joyful people I have known have been some who seem to have had no human reason for joy. The sweet fragrance of Christ has shown through their lives.

Elisabeth Elliot

A holy life will produce the deepest impression. Lighthouses blow no horns; they only shine.

D. L. Moody

Do you want to be counted wise, to build a reputation for wisdom? Here's what you do: Live well, live wisely, live humbly. It's the way you live, not the way you talk, that counts.

James 3:13 MSG

Today's Prayer

Lord, make me a worthy example to my family and friends. And, let my words and my deeds serve as a testimony to the changes You have made in my life. Let me praise You, Father, by following in the footsteps of Your Son, and let others see Him through me. Amen

When Mountains Need Moving

I assure you: If anyone says to this mountain,
"Be lifted up and thrown into the sea," and does not doubt
in his heart, but believes that what he says will happen,
it will be done for him.
Mark 11:23 HCSB

Because we live in a demanding world, all of us have mountains to climb and mountains to move. Moving those mountains requires faith.

Are you a mountain-moving parent whose faith is evident for all to see? Or, are you a spiritual underachiever? As you think about the answer to that question, consider this: God needs more people who are willing to move mountains for His glory and for His kingdom.

Every life—including yours—is a series of wins and losses. Every step of the way, through every triumph and tragedy, God walks with you, ready and willing to strengthen you. So the next time you find your courage tested to the limit, remember to take your fears to God. If you call upon Him, you will be comforted. Whatever your challenge, whatever your trouble, God can handle it.

When you place your faith, your trust, indeed your life in the hands of your Heavenly Father, you'll be amazed at the marvelous things He can do with you and through you. So strengthen your faith through praise, through worship, through Bible study, and through prayer. And trust God's plans. With Him, all things are possible, and He stands ready to open a world of possibilities to you . . . if you have faith.

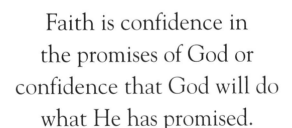

Faith is confidence in
the promises of God or
confidence that God will do
what He has promised.

—

Charles Stanley

I do not want merely to possess a faith; I want a faith that possesses me.

Charles Kingsley

Only God can move mountains, but faith and prayer can move God.

E. M. Bounds

Faith does not concern itself with the entire journey. One step is enough.

Mrs. Charles E. Cowman

Let us come near to God with a sincere heart and a sure faith, because we have been made free from a guilty conscience, and our bodies have been washed with pure water.

Hebrews 10:22 NCV

Today's Prayer

Dear Lord, I want faith that moves mountains. You have big plans for this world and big plans for me and my family. Help us fulfill those plans, Father, as we follow in the footsteps of Your Son. Amen

Beyond Anger

My dear brothers and sisters, be quick to listen,
slow to speak, and slow to get angry.
Your anger can never make things right in God's sight.
James 1:19-20 NLT

Parenting is vastly rewarding, but every parent knows that it can be, at times, frustrating. No family is perfect, and even the most loving parent's patience can, on occasion, wear thin.

Your temper is either your master or your servant. Either you control it, or it controls you. And the extent to which you allow anger to rule your life will determine, to a surprising degree, the quality of your relationships with others and your relationship with God.

Do you exercise firm control over your temper? Hopefully so. Temper tantrums are usually unproductive, unattractive, unforgettable, and unnecessary. Perhaps that's why Proverbs 16:32 states, "Controlling your temper is better than capturing a city" (NCV).

If you've allowed anger to become a regular visitor at your house, pray for wisdom, for patience, and for a heart that is so filled with love and forgiveness that it contains no room for bitterness. God will help you terminate your tantrums if you ask Him to. And God can help you perfect your ability to be a patient parent if you ask Him to. So ask Him, and then wait patiently for the ever-more-patient you to arrive.

Anger is the noise of the soul; the unseen irritant of the heart; the relentless invader of silence.

Max Lucado

When you strike out in anger, you may miss the other person, but you will always hit yourself.

Jim Gallery

But now you must also put away all the following: anger, wrath, malice, slander, and filthy language from your mouth.

Colossians 3:8 HCSB

Today's Prayer

Lord, sometimes, it is so easy to lose my temper and my perspective. When anger burdens my soul, enable me to calm myself and to be a witness to Your truth and righteousness. Let my children see me as a model of kindness and forgiveness, today and every day. Amen

---

Beyond Fear

I sought the Lord, and He answered me
and delivered me from all my fears.
Psalm 34:4 HCSB

We live in a world that is, at times, a frightening place. We live in a world that is, at times, a discouraging place. We live in a world where life-changing losses can be so painful and so profound that it seems we will never recover. But, with God's help, and with the help of encouraging family members and friends, we can recover.

During the darker days of life, we are wise to remember the words of Jesus, who reassured His disciples, saying, "Take courage! It is I. Don't be afraid" (Matthew 14:27 NIV). Then, with God's comfort and His love in our hearts, we can offer encouragement to others. And by helping them face their fears, we can, in turn, tackle our own problems with courage, determination, and faith.

Worry is a cycle of inefficient thoughts whirling around a center of fear.

Corrie ten Boom

When we meditate on God and remember the promises He has given us in His Word, our faith grows, and our fears dissolve.

Charles Stanley

One of the main missions of God is to free us from the debilitating bonds of fear and anxiety. God's heart is broken when He sees us so demoralized and weighed down by fear.

Bill Hybels

Even when I walk through the dark valley of death, I will not be afraid, for you are close beside me. Your rod and your staff protect and comfort me.

Psalm 23:4 NLT

Today's Prayer

Your Word reminds me, Lord, that even when I walk through the valley of the shadow of death, I need fear no evil, for You are with me, and You comfort me. Thank You, Lord, for a perfect love that casts out fear. Let me live courageously and faithfully this day and every day. Amen

He Is Sufficient

*And He said to me, "My grace is sufficient for you,
for My strength is made perfect in weakness."*
2 Corinthians 12:9 NKJV

Of this you can be certain: God is sufficient to meet your needs. Period.

Do the demands of parenting seem overwhelming at times? If so, you must learn to rely not only upon your own resources, but also upon the promises of your Father in heaven. God will hold your hand and walk with you and your family if you let Him. So even if your circumstances are difficult, trust the Father.

The Psalmist writes, "Weeping may endure for a night, but joy comes in the morning" (Psalm 30:5 NKJV). But when we are suffering, the morning may seem very far away. It is not. God promises that He is "near to those who have a broken heart" (Psalm 34:18 NKJV). When we are troubled, we must turn to Him, and we must encourage our friends and family members to do likewise.

If you are discouraged by the inevitable demands of life here on earth, be mindful of this fact: the loving heart of God is sufficient to meet any challenge . . . including yours.

The Rock of Ages is the great sheltering encirclement.

Oswald Chambers

Yes, God's grace is always sufficient, and His arms are always open to give it. But, will our arms be open to receive it?

Beth Moore

Under heaven's lock and key, we are protected by the most efficient security system available: the power of God.

Charles Swindoll

God's saints in all ages have realized that God was enough for them. God is enough for time; God is enough for eternity. God is enough!

Hannah Whitall Smith

I know whom I have believed and am persuaded that He is able to guard what has been entrusted to me until that day.

2 Timothy 1:12 HCSB

Today's Prayer

Dear Lord, as I face the challenges of this day, You protect me. I thank You, Father, for Your love and for Your strength. I will lean upon You today and forever. Amen

Choosing to Be Kind

*Our Father is kind; you be kind. Don't pick on people,
jump on their failures, criticize their faults—
unless, of course, you want the same treatment.
Don't condemn those who are down;
that hardness can boomerang.
Be easy on people; you'll find life a lot easier.*
Luke 6:36-37 MSG

Kindness is a choice. Sometimes, when we feel happy or generous, we find it easy to be kind. Other times, when we are discouraged or tired, we can scarcely summon the energy to utter a single kind word. But, God's commandment is clear: He intends that we make the conscious choice to treat others with kindness and respect, no matter our circumstances, no matter our emotions.

In the busyness and confusion of daily life, it is easy to lose focus, and it is easy to become frustrated. We are imperfect human beings struggling to manage our lives as best we can, but we often fall short. When we are distracted or disappointed, we may neglect to share a kind word or a kind deed. This oversight hurts others, but it hurts us most of all.

Today, slow yourself down and be alert for people who need your smile, your kind words, or your helping hand. Make kindness a centerpiece of your dealings with others. They will be blessed, and you will be too.

Sometimes one little spark of kindness is all it takes to reignite the light of hope in a heart that's blinded by pain.

Barbara Johnson

When you extend hospitality to others, you're not trying to impress people, you're trying to reflect God to them.

Max Lucado

A kind man benefits himself, but a cruel man brings disaster on himself.

Proverbs 11:17 HCSB

Today's Prayer

Lord, make me a loving, encouraging Christian parent. And, let my love for Christ be reflected through the kindness that I show to those who need the healing touch of the Master's hand. Amen

Getting to Know Him

Knowing God leads to self-control.
Self-control leads to patient endurance,
and patient endurance leads to godliness.

2 Peter 1:6 NLT

D o you ever wonder if God is really "right here, right now"? Do you wonder if God hears your prayers, if He understands your feelings, or if He really knows your heart? But when you have doubts, remember this: God isn't on a coffee break, and He hasn't moved out of town. He's right here, right now, listening to your thoughts and prayers, watching over your every move.

The Bible teaches that a wonderful way to get to know God is simply to be still and listen to Him. But sometimes, you may find it hard to slow down and listen. As the demands of everyday life weigh down upon you, you may be tempted to ignore God's presence or—worse yet—to rebel against His commandments. But, when you quiet yourself and acknowledge His presence, God touches your heart and restores your spirits. So why not let Him do it right now? If you really want to know Him better, silence is a wonderful place to start.

Slowly and surely, we learn
the great secret of life,
which is to know God.

—

Oswald Chambers

You cannot grow spiritually until you have the assurance that Christ is in your life.

Vonette Bright

Knowing God involves an intimate, personal relationship that is developed over time through prayer and getting answers to prayer, through Bible study and applying its teaching to our lives, through obedience and experiencing the power of God, through moment-by-moment submission to Him that results in a moment-by-moment filling of the Holy Spirit.

Anne Graham Lotz

Here is our opportunity: we cannot see God, but we can see Christ. Christ was not only the Son of God, but He was the Father. Whatever Christ was, that God is.

Hannah Whitall Smith

The one who does not love does not know God, because God is love.

1 John 4:8 HCSB

Today's Prayer

Dear Lord, help me remember the importance of silence. Help me discover quiet moments throughout the day so that I can sense Your presence and Your love. Amen

---

Making Peace with the Past

Do not remember the past events,
pay no attention to things of old. Look,
I am about to do something new; even now it is coming.
Do you not see it? Indeed, I will make a way
in the wilderness, rivers in the desert.
Isaiah 43:18-19 HCSB

Are you a parent who's made peace with your past? If so, congratulations. But, if you are mired in the quicksand of regret, it's time to plan your escape. How can you do so? By accepting what has been and by trusting God for what will be.

Because you are human, you may be slow to forget yesterday's disappointments; if so you are not alone. But if you sincerely seek to focus your hopes and energies on the future, then you must find ways to accept the past, no matter how difficult it may be to do so.

If you have not yet made peace with the past, today is the day to declare an end to all hostilities. When you do, you can then turn your thoughts to the wondrous promises of God and to the glorious future that He has in store for you.

Shake the dust from your past, and move forward in His promises.

Kay Arthur

Whoever you are, whatever your condition or circumstance, whatever your past or problem, Jesus can restore you to wholeness.

Anne Graham Lotz

Yesterday is just experience but tomorrow is glistening with purpose—and today is the channel leading from one to the other.

Barbara Johnson

I do not consider myself yet to have taken hold of it. But one thing I do: Forgetting what is behind and straining toward what is ahead, I press on toward the goal to win the prize for which God has called me heavenward in Christ Jesus.

Philippians 3:13-14 NIV

Today's Prayer

Heavenly Father, free me from anger, resentment, and envy. When I am bitter, I cannot feel the peace that You intend for my life. Keep me mindful that forgiveness is Your commandment, and help me accept the past, treasure the present, and trust the future . . . to You. Amen

So Laugh!

Laugh with your happy friends when they're happy;
share tears when they're down.
Romans 12:15 MSG

Laughter is a gift from God, a gift that He intends for us to use. Yet sometimes, because of the inevitable stresses of everyday living, we fail to find the fun in life. When we allow life's inevitable disappointments to cast a pall over our lives and our souls, we do a profound disservice to ourselves and to our loved ones.

If you've allowed the clouds of life to obscure the blessings of life, perhaps you've formed the unfortunate habit of taking things just a little too seriously. If so, it's time to fret a little less and laugh a little more.

So today, look for the humor that most certainly surrounds you—when you do, you'll find it. And remember: God created laughter for a reason . . . and Father indeed knows best. So laugh!

As you're rushing through life, take time to stop a moment, look into people's eyes, say something kind, and try to make them laugh!

Barbara Johnson

I think everybody ought to be a laughing Christian. I'm convinced that there's just one place where there's not any laughter, and that's hell.

Jerry Clower

If you want people to feel comfortable around you, to enjoy being with you, then learn to laugh at yourself and find humor in life's little mishaps.

Dennis Swanberg

There is a time for everything, and everything on earth has its special season. . . . There is a time to cry and a time to laugh. There is a time to be sad and a time to dance.

Ecclesiastes 3:1, 4 NCV

Today's Prayer

Lord, when I begin to take myself or my life too seriously, let me laugh. When I rush from place to place, slow me down, Lord, and let me laugh. Put a smile on my face, Dear Lord, and let me share that smile with all who cross my path . . . and let me laugh. Amen

---

Lifetime Learning

Start with God—the first step in learning
is bowing down to God.
Proverbs 1:7 MSG

When it comes to learning life's lessons, we can either do things the easy way or the hard way. The easy way can be summed up as follows: when God teaches us a lesson, we learn it . . . the first time! Unfortunately, too many of us—both parents and children alike—learn much more slowly than that.

When we resist God's instruction, He continues to teach, whether we like it or not. And if we keep making the same old mistakes, God responds by rewarding us with the same old results.

Our challenge, then, is to discern God's lessons from the experiences of everyday life. Hopefully, we learn those lessons sooner rather than later because the sooner we do, the sooner He can move on to the next lesson and the next and the next . . .

The wonderful thing about God's schoolroom is that we get to grade our own papers. You see, He doesn't test us so He can learn how well we're doing. He tests us so we can discover how well we're doing.

Charles Swindoll

Today is yesterday's pupil.

Thomas Fuller

True learning can take place at every age of life, and it doesn't have to be in the curriculum plan.

Suzanne Dale Ezell

While chastening is always difficult, if we look to God for the lesson we should learn, we will see spiritual fruit.

Vonette Bright

Remember what you are taught, and listen carefully to words of knowledge.

Proverbs 23:12 NCV

Today's Prayer

Dear Lord, I have so much to learn. Help me to watch, to listen, to think, and to learn, every day of my life. Amen

Your Wonderful Life

*For whoever finds me finds life
and receives favor from the LORD.*
Proverbs 8:35 NIV

Each day, as we awaken from sleep and begin the new day, we are confronted with countless opportunities to serve God and to worship Him. When we do, He blesses us. But, if we turn our backs to the Creator, or, if we are simply too busy to acknowledge His greatness, we do ourselves a profound disservice.

As parents in a fast-changing world, we face challenges that sometimes leave us feeling overworked, overcommitted, and overwhelmed. But God has different plans for us. He intends that we take time each day to slow down long enough to praise Him and glorify His Son. When we do, our spirits are calmed and our lives are enriched, as are the lives of our families and friends.

Each day provides a glorious opportunity to place ourselves in the service of the One who is the Giver of all blessings. May we seek His will, trust His word, and place Him where He belongs: at the center of our lives.

The Christian life is motivated, not by a list of do's and don'ts, but by the gracious outpouring of God's love and blessing.

Anne Graham Lotz

Life is simply hard. That's all there is to it. Thank goodness, the intensity of difficulty rises and falls. Some seasons are far more bearable than others, but none is without challenge.

Beth Moore

People, places, and things were never meant to give us life. God alone is the author of a fulfilling life.

Gary Smalley & John Trent

I have set before you life and death, blessings and curses. Now choose life, so that you and your children may live and that you may love the LORD your God, listen to his voice, and hold fast to him.

Deuteronomy 30:19-20 NIV

Today's Prayer

Lord, You have given me the gift of life. Let me treasure it, and let me use it for Your service and for Your glory. Amen

Listen Carefully

The one who is from God listens to God's words.
This is why you don't listen,
because you are not from God.
John 8:47 HCSB

Sometimes God speaks loudly and clearly. More often, He speaks in a quiet voice—and if you are wise, you will be listening carefully when He does. To do so, you must carve out quiet moments each day to study His Word and sense His direction.

Can you quiet yourself long enough to listen to your conscience? Are you attuned to the subtle guidance of your intuition? Are you willing to pray sincerely and then to wait quietly for God's response? Hopefully so. Usually God refrains from sending His messages on stone tablets or city billboards. More often, He communicates in subtler ways. If you sincerely desire to hear His voice, you must listen carefully, and you must do so in the silent corners of your quiet, willing heart.

In the soul-searching of our lives, we are to stay quiet so we can hear Him say all that He wants to say to us in our hearts.

Charles Swindoll

Listening is loving.

Zig Ziglar

We cannot experience the fullness of Christ if we do all the expressing. We must allow God to express His love, will, and truth to us.

Gary Smalley

When we come to Jesus stripped of pretensions, with a needy spirit, ready to listen, He meets us at the point of need.

Catherine Marshall

Be still, and know that I am God.

Psalm 46:10 KJV

Today's Prayer

Lord, give me the wisdom to be a good listener. Help me listen carefully to my family, to my friends, and—most importantly—to You. Amen

A Parent's Love

Now these three remain: faith, hope, and love.
But the greatest of these is love.
1 Corinthians 13:13 HCSB

The familiar words of 1st Corinthians 13 remind us of the importance of love. Faith is important, of course. So, too, is hope. But love is more important still. Christ showed His love for us on the cross, and, as Christians, we are called upon to return Christ's love by sharing it. We are commanded (not advised, not encouraged . . . commanded!) to love one another just as Christ loved us (John 13:34). That's a tall order, but as Christians, we are obligated to follow it.

Sometimes love is easy (puppies and sleeping children come to mind), and sometimes love is hard (fallible human beings come to mind). But God's Word is clear: We are to love our families and our neighbors without reservation or condition.

As a Christian parent, you are charged with a profound responsibility: the job of raising your child with love, discernment, and discipline. When you create a loving home for your clan, a home that honors God and mirrors His love, you are giving your family the greatest gift this side of heaven. So today, take the time to make certain your loved ones know they're loved. And while you're at it, be sure to spread Christ's message by word and by example. And, of course, the greatest of these is example.

When it comes to raising our kids, 1 Corinthians 13:13 certainly applies: The "greatest of these" is, indeed, love. Every child deserves to grow up in a safe, loving, God-fearing home, and it's up to you to make certain that your home fits that description.

Homes that are built on anything other than love are bound to crumble.

—

Billy Graham

It is when we come to the Lord in our nothingness, our powerlessness and our helplessness that He then enables us to love in a way which, without Him, would be absolutely impossible.

Elisabeth Elliot

Love is extravagant in the price it is willing to pay, the time it is willing to give, the hardships it is willing to endure, and the strength it is willing to spend. Love never thinks in terms of "how little," but always in terms of "how much." Love gives, love knows, and love lasts.

Joni Eareckson Tada

This is my command: Love one another the way I loved you. This is the very best way to love. Put your life on the line for your friends.

John 15:12-13 MSG

Today's Prayer

Dear Lord, today and every day, I will tell my family that I love them. And I will show my family that I love them. Amen

Beyond Materialism

*Don't collect for yourselves treasures on earth, where moth
and rust destroy and where thieves break in and steal.
But collect for yourselves treasures in heaven, where neither
moth nor rust destroys, and where thieves don't break in and
steal. For where your treasure is, there your heart will be also.*
Matthew 6:19-21 HCSB

In our modern society, we need money to live. But as Christians, we must never make the acquisition of money the central focus of our lives. Money is a tool, but it should never overwhelm our sensibilities. The focus of life must be squarely on things spiritual, not things material.

Whenever we place our love for material possessions above our love for God—or when we yield to the countless other temptations of everyday living—we find ourselves engaged in a struggle between good and evil, a clash between God and Satan. Our responses to these struggles have implications that echo throughout our families and throughout our communities. Let us choose wisely by freeing ourselves from that subtle yet powerful temptation: the temptation to love the world more than we love God.

When possessions become our god, we become materialistic and greedy . . . and we forfeit our contentment and our joy.

Charles Swindoll

If you want to be truly happy, you won't find it on an endless quest for more stuff. You'll find it in receiving God's generosity and then passing that generosity along.

Bill Hybels

It's sobering to contemplate how much time, effort, sacrifice, compromise, and attention we give to acquiring and increasing our supply of something that is totally insignificant in eternity.

Anne Graham Lotz

No one can serve two masters. The person will hate one master and love the other, or will follow one master and refuse to follow the other. You cannot serve both God and worldly riches.

Matthew 6:24 NCV

Today's Prayer

Dear Lord, keep me mindful that material possessions cannot bring me joy—my joy comes from You. I will share that joy with family, with friends, and with neighbors, this day and every day. Amen

Media Messages

Set your minds on what is above, not on what is on the earth.
Colossians 3:2 HCSB

If you and your loved ones have acquired the bad habit of watching whatever happens to pop up on you family's TV screen, it's time to rethink the way you control your clicker. Most television networks (as well as the other forms of popular media) can be dangerous to your emotional and spiritual health.

The media is working around the clock in an attempt to rearrange your family's priorities in ways that are definitely not in your best interests. The media is trying to teach your family that physical appearance is all-important, that material possessions should be acquired at any cost, and that the world operates independently of God's laws. But guess what? Those messages are lies.

In the pursuit of profits, the media glamorizes violence, exploits suffering, and sensationalizes sex, all in the name of "ratings" (translated: "money").

So here's a question for you and your family: Will you control what appears on your TV screen, or will you be controlled by it? If you're willing to take complete control over the images that appear inside the four walls of your home, you'll be doing yourselves a king-sized favor. So forget the media hype, and pay attention to God. Stand up for Him and be counted, not just in church where it's relatively easy to be a Christian, but also when you're deciding what to watch. You owe it to your Creator . . . and you owe it to yourselves.

———————————————

The more we stuff ourselves
with material pleasures,
the less we seem to appreciate life.

—

Barbara Johnson

As we have by faith said no to sin, so we should by faith say yes to God and set our minds on things above, where Christ is seated in the heavenlies.

Vonette Bright

Our fight is not against any physical enemy; it is against organizations and powers that are spiritual. We must struggle against sin all our lives, but we are assured we will win.

Corrie ten Boom

Do not love the world or the things that belong to the world. If anyone loves the world, love for the Father is not in him. Because everything that belongs to the world—the lust of the flesh, the lust of the eyes, and the pride in one's lifestyle—is not from the Father, but is from the world.

1 John 2:15-16 HCSB

Today's Prayer

Dear Lord, I am an imperfect human being living in an imperfect world. Direct my path far from the temptations and distractions of this world, and let me follow in the footsteps of Your Son today and forever. Amen

Do You Believe in Miracles?

You are the God who performs miracles;
you display your power among the peoples.
Psalm 77:14 NIV

Do you believe that God is at work in the world? And do you also believe that nothing is impossible for Him? If so, then you also believe that God is perfectly capable of doing things that you, as a mere human being with limited vision and limited understanding, would deem to be utterly impossible. And that's precisely what God does.

Since the moment that He created our universe out of nothingness, God has made a habit of doing miraculous things. And He still works miracles today. Expect Him to work miracles in your own life and in the lives of your loved ones. Then be watchful. With God, absolutely nothing is impossible, including an amazing assortment of miracles that He stands ready, willing, and able to perform for you and yours.

God specializes in things thought impossible.

Catherine Marshall

Miracles are not contrary to nature but only contrary to what we know about nature.

St. Augustine

Only God can move mountains, but faith and prayer can move God.

E. M. Bounds

Too many Christians live below the miracle level.

Vance Havner

With God's power working in us, God can do much, much more than anything we can ask or imagine.

Ephesians 3:20 NCV

Today's Prayer

Lord, for You, nothing is impossible. Let me trust in Your power to do the miraculous, and let me trust in Your willingness to work miracles in my life—and in my heart. Amen

Ignoring Sin

For everyone who practices wicked things hates the light and
avoids it, so that his deeds may not be exposed.
But anyone who lives by the truth comes to the light,
so that his works may be shown to be accomplished by God.
John 3:20–21 HCSB

If we deny our sins, we allow those sins to flourish. And if we allow sinful behaviors to become habits, we invite hardships into our own lives and into the lives of our loved ones. When we yield to the distractions and temptations of this troubled world, we suffer. But God has other intentions, and His plans for our lives do not include sin or denial.

When we allow ourselves to encounter God's presence, He will lead us away from temptation, away from confusion, and away from the self-deception. God is the champion of truth and the enemy of denial. May we see ourselves through His eyes and conduct ourselves accordingly.

Unconfessed sin in your life will cause you to doubt.

Anne Graham Lotz

What I like about experience is that it is such an honest thing. You may take any number of wrong turnings; but keep your eyes open and you will not be allowed to go very far before the warning signs appear. You may have deceived yourself, but experience is not trying to deceive you. The universe rings true wherever you fairly test it.

C. S. Lewis

We cannot out-sin God's ability to forgive us.

Beth Moore

Disaster pursues sinners, but good rewards the righteous.

Proverbs 13:21 HCSB

Today's Prayer

Dear Lord, when I displease You, I do injury to myself, to my family, and to my community. Because sin distances me from You, Lord, I will fear sin and I will avoid sinful places. The fear of sinning against You is a healthy fear, Father, because it can motivate me to accomplish Your will. Let a healthy fear of sin guide my path, today and every day of my life. Amen

Obedience Now

*For God is working in you, giving you the desire
to obey him and the power to do what pleases him.*
Philippians 2:13 NLT

As loving parents, we must teach our children to obey the rules of society and the laws of God. God's laws are contained in a guidebook for righteous living called the Holy Bible. It contains thorough instructions which, if followed, lead to fulfillment, peace, righteousness, and salvation. But, if we choose to ignore God's commandments, the results are as predictable as they are tragic.

Talking about obedience is easy; living obediently is considerably harder. But, if we are to be responsible role models for our families and friends, we must study God's Word and obey it.

Phillips Brooks advised, "Be such a person, and live such a life, that if every person were such as you, and every life a life like yours, this earth would be God's Paradise." And that's sound advice because our families and friends are watching . . . and so, for that matter, is God.

Obedience is the outward expression of your love of God.

Henry Blackaby

God is God. Because He is God, He is worthy of my trust and obedience. I will find rest nowhere but in His holy will, a will that is unspeakably beyond my largest notions of what He is up to.

Elisabeth Elliot

The pathway of obedience can sometimes be difficult, but it always leads to a strengthening of our inner self.

Vonette Bright

Not everyone who says to Me, "Lord, Lord!" will enter the kingdom of heaven, but the one who does the will of My Father in heaven.

Matthew 7:21 HCSB

Today's Prayer

Dear Lord, make me a parent who is obedient to Your Word. Let me live according to Your commandments. Direct my path far from the temptations and distractions of this world. And, let me discover Your will and follow it, Lord, this day and always. Amen

Share Your Optimism

*My cup runs over. Surely goodness and mercy
shall follow me all the days of my life;
and I will dwell in the house of the Lord Forever.*
Psalm 23:5-6 NKJV

Because you are a conscientious parent living in a difficult world, you may find yourself pulled down by the inevitable demands and worries of everyday life in the 21st century. Ours is a world brimming with temptations, distractions, and dangers. Sometimes, we can't help ourselves: we worry for our families, and we worry for ourselves.

If you become discouraged, exhausted, or both, then it's time to take your concerns to God. Whether you find yourself at the pinnacle of the mountain or the darkest depths of the valley, God is there. Open your heart to Him and He will lift your spirits and renew your strength.

Today, as a gift to your family and yourself, why not claim the joy that is rightfully yours in Christ? Why not take time to celebrate God's glorious creation? Why not trust your hopes instead of your fears? When you do, you will think optimistically about yourself and your world . . .

and you can then share your optimism with others. They'll be better for it, and so will you. But not necessarily in that order.

Make the least of all that goes and the most of all that comes. Don't regret what is past. Cherish what you have. Look forward to all that is to come. And most important of all, rely moment by moment on Jesus Christ.

Gigi Graham Tchividjian

Christ can put a spring in your step and a thrill in your heart. Optimism and cheerfulness are products of knowing Christ.

Billy Graham

I can do everything through him that gives me strength.

Philippians 4:13 NIV

Today's Prayer

Dear Lord, I will look for the best in other people, I will expect the best from You, and I will try my best to do my best—today and every day. Amen

---

God's Timetable

He has made everything beautiful in its time.
He has also set eternity in the hearts of men;
yet they cannot fathom what God has done
from beginning to end.

Ecclesiastes 3:11 NIV

Are you anxious for God to work out His plans for you and your loved ones? Who isn't? As believers, we all want God to do great things for us and through us, and we want Him to do those things now. But sometimes, God has other plans. Sometimes, God's timetable does not coincide with our own. It's worth noting, however, that God's timetable is always perfect.

The next time you find your patience tested to the limit, remember that the world unfolds according to God's plan, not ours. Sometimes, we must wait patiently, and that's as it should be. After all, think how patient God has been with us.

God has a designated time when his promise will be fulfilled and the prayer will be answered.

Jim Cymbala

God is in no hurry. Compared to the works of mankind, He is extremely deliberate. God is not a slave to the human clock.

Charles Swindoll

When there is perplexity there is always guidance—not always at the moment we ask, but in good time, which is God's time. There is no need to fret and stew.

Elisabeth Elliot

Wait for the Lord; be courageous and let your heart be strong. Wait for the Lord.

Psalm 27:14 HCSB

Today's Prayer

Dear Lord, Your wisdom is infinite, and the timing of Your heavenly plan is perfect. You have a plan for my life that is grander than I can imagine. When I am impatient, remind me that You are never early or late. You are always on time, Father, so let me trust in You. Amen

The Wisdom to Be Grateful

Let the message about the Messiah dwell richly among you,
teaching and admonishing one another in all wisdom,
and singing psalms, hymns, and spiritual songs,
with gratitude in your hearts to God.
Colossians 3:16 HCSB

For most of us, life is busy and complicated. We have countless responsibilities, some of which begin before sunrise and many of which end long after sunset. Amid the rush and crush of the daily grind, it is easy to lose sight of God and His blessings. But, when we forget to slow down and say "Thank You" to our Maker, we rob ourselves of His presence, His peace, and His joy.

Our task—as the leaders of our families and as believing Christians—is to praise God many times each day. Then, with gratitude in our hearts, we can face our daily duties with the perspective and power that only He can provide.

A sense of gratitude for God's presence in our lives will help open our eyes to what he has done in the past and what he will do in the future.

Emilie Barnes

Gratitude changes the pangs of memory into a tranquil joy.

Dietrich Bonhoeffer

We become happy, spiritually prosperous people not because we receive what we want, but because we appreciate what we have.

Penelope Stokes

Therefore, since we receive a kingdom which cannot be shaken, let us show gratitude, by which we may offer to God an acceptable service with reverence and awe . . . .

Hebrews 12:28 NASB

Today's Prayer

Lord, let my attitude be one of gratitude. You have given me much; when I think of Your grace and goodness, I am humbled and thankful. Today, let me express my thanksgiving, Father, not just through my words but also through my deeds . . . and may all the glory be Yours. Amen

Healthy Habits

*Whatever you eat or drink or whatever you do,
you must do all for the glory of God.*
1 Corinthians 10:31 NLT

It's an old saying and a true one: First, you make your habits, and then your habits make you. Some habits will inevitably bring you closer to God; other habits will lead you away from the path He has chosen for you. If you sincerely desire to improve your spiritual health, you must honestly examine the habits that make up the fabric of your day. And you must abandon those habits that are displeasing to God.

If you trust God, and if you keep asking for His help, He can transform your life. If you sincerely ask Him to help you, the same God who created the universe will help you defeat the harmful habits that have heretofore defeated you. So, if at first you don't succeed, keep praying. God is listening, and He's ready to help you become a better person if you ask Him . . . so ask today.

You will never change your life until you change something you do daily.

John Maxwell

The simple fact is that if we sow a lifestyle that is in direct disobedience to God's reveled Word, we ultimately reap disaster.

Charles Swindoll

Since behaviors become habits, make them work with you and not against you.

E. Stanley Jones

Prayer is a habit. Worship is a habit. Kindness is a habit. And if you want to please God, you'd better make sure that these habits are your habits.

Marie T. Freeman

Do not be deceived: "Evil company corrupts good habits."
1 Corinthians 15:33 NKJV

Today's Prayer

Dear Lord, help me break bad habits and form good ones. And let my actions be pleasing to You, today and every day. Amen

Happiness Now

But happy are those . . .
whose hope is in the LORD their God.
Psalm 146:5 NLT

Okay, it's been a typical day. You've cared for your family, worked your fingers to the bone, rushed from Point A to Point Z, and taken barely a moment for yourself. But have you taken time to smile? If so, you're a very wise parent. If not, it's time to slow down, to take a deep breath, and to recount your blessings!

God has promised all of us the opportunity to experience spiritual abundance and peace. But it's up to each of us to claim the spiritual riches that God has in store. God promises us a life of fulfillment and joy, but He does not force His joy upon us.

Would you like to experience the peace and the joy that God intends for you? Then accept His Son and lay claim to His promises. And then, put a smile on your face that stretches all the way down to your heart. When you do, you'll discover that when you smile at God, He smiles back.

Christ is the secret, the source, the substance, the center, and the circumference of all true and lasting gladness.

Mrs. Charles E. Cowman

Our thoughts, not our circumstances, determine our happiness.

John Maxwell

I became aware of one very important concept I had missed before: my attitude—not my circumstances—was what was making me unhappy.

Vonette Bright

Happy are the people whose strength is in You, whose hearts are set on pilgrimage.

Psalm 84:5 HCSB

Today's Prayer

Lord, let me be a parent who celebrates life. Let me rejoice in the gift of this day, and let me praise You for the gift of Your Son. Let me be a joyful Christian, Lord, as I share Your Good News with friends, with family, and with the world. Amen

---

The Best Policy

*Better to be poor and honest
than a rich person no one can trust.*
Proverbs 19:1 MSG

It has been said on many occasions and in many ways that honesty is the best policy. For believers, it is far more important to note that honesty is God's policy. And if we are to be servants worthy of Jesus Christ, we must be honest and forthright in our communications with others. Sometimes, honesty is difficult; sometimes, honesty is painful; sometimes, honesty is inconvenient; but always honesty is God's commandment.

In the Book of Proverbs, we read, "The Lord detests lying lips, but he delights in men who are truthful" (12:22 NIV). Clearly, we must strive to be parents whose words are pleasing to our Creator. Truth is God's way, and it must be our way, too, even when telling the truth is difficult. As loving parents, we should do no less.

Integrity is not a given factor in everyone's life. It is a result of self-discipline, inner trust, and a decision to be relentlessly honest in all situations in our lives.

John Maxwell

God doesn't expect you to be perfect, but he does insist on complete honesty.

Rick Warren

The single most important element in any human relationship is honesty—with oneself, with God, and with others.

Catherine Marshall

The honest person will live in safety, but the dishonest will be caught.

Proverbs 10:9 NCV

Today's Prayer

Heavenly Father, You instruct Your children to seek truth and to live righteously. Help me always to live according to Your commandments. Sometimes, Lord, speaking the truth is difficult, but let me always speak truthfully and forthrightly. And, let me walk righteously and courageously so that others might see Your grace reflected in my words and my deeds. Amen

Finding Hope

*Now may the God of hope fill you with all joy
and peace in believing, so that you may overflow with hope
by the power of the Holy Spirit.*

Romans 15:13 HCSB

Are you a hope-filled parent? You should be. After all, God is good; His love endures; and He has offered you the priceless gift of eternal life. And, of course, God has blessed you with a loving family. But sometimes, in life's darker moments, you may lose sight of those blessings, and when you do, it's easy to lose hope.

When a suffering woman sought healing by merely touching the hem of His cloak, Jesus replied, "Daughter, be of good comfort; thy faith hath made thee whole" (Matthew 9:22 KJV). The message to believers is clear: if we are to be made whole by God, we must live by faith.

If you find yourself falling into the spiritual traps of worry and discouragement, seek the healing touch of Jesus and the encouraging words of fellow Christians. This world can be a place of trials and tribulations, but as believers, we are secure. Our hope is in God; He has promised us peace, joy, and eternal life. And, of course, God keeps His promises today, tomorrow, and forever, amen!

The hope we have in Jesus is the anchor for the soul—something sure and steadfast, preventing drifting or giving way, lowered to the depth of God's love.

Franklin Graham

Love is the seed of all hope. It is the enticement to trust, to risk, to try, and to go on.

Gloria Gaither

Faith looks back and draws courage; hope looks ahead and keeps desire alive.

John Eldredge

This hope we have as an anchor of the soul, a hope both sure and steadfast.

Hebrews 6:19 NASB

Today's Prayer

Today, Dear Lord, I will live in hope. If I become discouraged, I will turn to You. If I grow weary, I will seek strength in You. In every aspect of my life, I will trust You. You are my Father, Lord, and I place my hope and my faith in You. Amen

The Wisdom to Be Humble

God has chosen you and made you his holy people.
He loves you. So always do these things:
Show mercy to others, be kind, humble, gentle, and patient.
Colossians 3:12 NCV

Hopefully, you are a proud parent. God intends that you take appropriate parental pride in every member of your family. But God has a stern warning for those who would take undo pride in their own accomplishments. Excessive pride is a sin.

As Christians, we have a profound reason to be humble: We have been refashioned and saved by Jesus Christ, and that salvation came not because of our own good works but because of God's grace. Thus, we are not "self-made"; we are "God-made" and "Christ-saved." How, then, can we be boastful? The answer, of course, is simple: if we are to be honest with ourselves and with our God, we cannot be boastful. In the quiet moments, when we search the depths of our own hearts, we know that whatever "it" is, God did that. And He deserves the credit.

Humility is not thinking
less of yourself;
it is thinking of yourself less.

—

Rick Warren

God exalts humility. When God works in our lives, helping us to become humble, he gives us a permanent joy. Humility gives us a joy that cannot be taken away.

Max Lucado

It was pride that changed angels into devils; it is humility that makes men as angels.

St. Augustine

If you know who you are in Christ, your personal ego is not an issue.

Beth Moore

For everyone who exalts himself will be humbled, and the one who humbles himself will be exalted.

Luke 14:11 HCSB

Today's Prayer

Heavenly Father, Jesus clothed Himself with humility when He chose to leave heaven and come to earth to live and die for us, His children. Christ is my Master and my example. Clothe me with humility, Lord, so that I might be more like Your Son, and keep me mindful that You are the giver and sustainer of life, and to You, Dear Lord, goes the glory and the praise. Amen

Imitating the Master

Therefore, be imitators of God,
as dearly loved children.
Ephesians 5:1 HCSB

Imitating Christ is impossible, but attempting to imitate Him is both possible and advisable. By attempting to imitate Jesus, we seek, to the best of our abilities, to walk in His footsteps. To the extent we succeed in following Him, we receive the spiritual abundance that is the rightful possession of those who love Christ and keep His commandments.

Do you seek God's blessings for the day ahead? Then, to the best of your abilities, imitate His Son. You will fall short, of course. But if your heart is right and your intentions are pure, God will bless your efforts, your day, and your life.

Christlikeness is not produced by imitation, but by inhabitation.

Rick Warren

Every Christian is to become a little Christ. The whole purpose of becoming a Christian is simply nothing else.

C. S. Lewis

A person who gazes and keeps on gazing at Jesus becomes like him in appearance.

E. Stanley Jones

Jesus answered, "If people love me, they will obey my teaching. My Father will love them, and we will come to them and make our home with them."

John 14:23 NCV

Today's Prayer

Dear Jesus, because I am Your disciple, I will trust You, I will obey Your teachings, and I will share Your Good News. You have given me life abundant and life eternal, and I will follow You today and forever. Amen

Real Joy

I've told you these things for a purpose:
that my joy might be your joy, and your joy wholly mature.
John 15:11 MSG

A re you a parent whose smile is evident for all to see? If so, congratulations: your joyful spirit serves as a powerful example to your family and friends. And because of your attitude, you may be assured that your children will indeed "rise up" and call you blessed (Proverbs 31:28).

Sometimes, amid the inevitable hustle and bustle of life here on earth, you may forfeit—albeit temporarily—the joy that God intends for you to experience and to share. But even on life's most difficult days, you may rest assured that God is in His heaven, and He still cares for you.

God's plan for you and your family includes heaping helpings of abundance and joy. Claim them. And remember that Christ offers you and your family priceless gifts: His abundance, His peace, and His joy. Accept those gifts and share them freely, just as Christ has freely shared Himself with you.

When I met Christ,
I felt that I had swallowed
sunshine.

—

E. Stanley Jones

Joy comes from knowing God loves me and knows who I am and where I'm going . . . that my future is secure as I rest in Him.

James Dobson

I choose joy. I will refuse the temptation to be cynical; cynicism is the tool of a lazy thinker. I will refuse to see people as anything less than human beings, created by God. I will refuse to see any problem as anything less than an opportunity to see God.

Max Lucado

The Christian lifestyle is not one of legalistic do's and don'ts, but one that is positive, attractive, and joyful.

Vonette Bright

A joyful heart is good medicine, but a broken spirit dries up the bones.

Proverbs 17:22 NASB

Today's Prayer

Dear Lord, You have blessed me with a loving family; make me thankful, loving, responsible, and wise. I praise You, Father, for the gift of Your Son and for the gift of salvation. Let me be a joyful Christian and a worthy example, this day and every day that I live. Amen

The Power of Patience

Be gentle to everyone, able to teach, and patient.
2 Timothy 2:23 HCSB

The rigors of parenting can test the patience of the most even-tempered moms and dads. From time to time, even the most mannerly children may do things that worry us, confuse us, or anger us. Why? Because they are children and because they are human. As loving parents, we must be patient with our children's shortcomings (just as they, too, must be patient with ours).

Proverbs 19:11 makes it clear: "People with good sense restrain their anger; they earn esteem by overlooking wrongs" (NLT). Sometimes, patience is the price we pay for being responsible parent, and that's as it should be. After all, think how patient our Heavenly Father has been with us.

The only person who doesn't need patience is the one who can control all the people and circumstances in life—and no such person exists.

Warren Wiersbe

Be patient and understanding. Life is too short to be vengeful or malicious.

Phillips Brooks

The next time you're disappointed, don't panic. Don't give up. Just be patient and let God remind you he's still in control.

Max Lucado

A patient person [shows] great understanding, but a quick-tempered one promotes foolishness.

Proverbs 14:29 HCSB

Today's Prayer

Heavenly Father, let me wait quietly for You. Let me live according to Your plan and according to Your timetable. When I am hurried, slow me down. When I become impatient with others, give me empathy. Today, I want to be a patient Christian, Dear Lord, as I trust in You and in Your master plan. Amen

Accepting His Peace

*And the peace of God, which surpasses all comprehension,
will guard your hearts and your minds in Christ Jesus.*
Philippians 4:7 NASB

As a busy parent, your plate is probably full: kids to care for, bills to pay, a home to manage. Sometimes it seems that you can scarcely find a moment's peace. But the beautiful words of John 14:27 are a reminder that God's peace is always available to you.

Jesus said, "Peace I leave with you, my peace I give unto you . . . ." Christ offers us peace, not as the world gives, but as He alone gives. We, as believers, can accept His peace or ignore it.

When we accept the peace of Jesus Christ into our hearts, our lives are transformed. And then, because we possess the gift of peace, we can share that gift with fellow Christians, family members, friends, and associates. If, on the other hand, we choose to ignore the gift of peace—for whatever reason—we simply cannot share what we do not possess.

Today, as a gift to yourself, to your family, and to your friends, claim the inner peace that is your spiritual birthright: the peace of Jesus Christ. It is offered freely; it has been paid for in full; it is yours for the asking. So ask. And then share.

A great many people are trying to make peace, but that has already been done. God has not left it for us to do; all we have to do is to enter into it.

D. L. Moody

The fruit of our placing all things in God's hands is the presence of His abiding peace in our hearts.

Hannah Whitall Smith

May the God of hope fill you with all joy and peace as you trust in him, so that you may overflow with hope by the power of the Holy Spirit.

Romans 15:13 NIV

Today's Prayer

Dear Lord, the peace that the world offers is fleeting, but You offer a peace that is perfect and eternal. Let me take my concerns and burdens to You, Father, and let me feel the spiritual abundance that You offer through the person of Your Son, the Prince of Peace. Amen

The Power of Perseverance

I have fought the good fight, I have finished the race,
I have kept the faith.

2 Timothy 4:7 HCSB

Someone once said, "Life is a marathon, not a sprint." The same can be said for parenting. Parenting requires courage, perseverance, determination, and, of course, an unending supply of love.

Every family and every life has its share of roadblocks and stumbling blocks; these situations require courage and determination. As an example of perfect courage and steadfast determination, we need look no further than our Savior, Jesus Christ.

Are you tired? Ask God for strength. Are you discouraged? Believe in His promises. Are you frustrated or fearful? Pray as if everything depended upon God, and work as if everything depended upon you. With God's help, you will find the strength to be the kind of parent who makes the Heavenly Father beam with pride.

By perseverance
the snail reached the ark.

—

C. H. Spurgeon

Perseverance is more than endurance. It is endurance combined with absolute assurance and certainty that what we are looking for is going to happen.

Oswald Chambers

Failure is one of life's most powerful teachers. How we handle our failures determines whether we're going to simply "get by" in life or "press on."

Beth Moore

Battles are won in the trenches, in the grit and grime of courageous determination; they are won day by day in the arena of life.

Charles Swindoll

For you need endurance, so that after you have done God's will, you may receive what was promised.

Hebrews 10:36 HCSB

Today's Prayer

Dear Lord, when my responsibilities as a parent seem overwhelming, slow me down and give me perspective. Keep me steady and sure. When I become weary, let me persevere so that, in Your time, I might finish my work here on earth, and that You might then say, "Well done my good and faithful servant." Amen

Keeping a Proper Perspective

Since you have been raised to new life with Christ,
set your sights on the realities of heaven, where Christ sits
at God's right hand in the place of honor and power.

Colossians 3:1 NLT

Even if you're the world's most thoughtful parent, you may, from time to time, lose perspective—it happens on those days when life seems out of balance and the pressures of parenting seem overwhelming. What's needed is a fresh perspective, a restored sense of balance . . . and God.

If a temporary loss of perspective has left you worried, exhausted, or both, it's time to readjust your thought patterns. Negative thoughts are habit-forming; thankfully, so are positive ones. With practice, you can form the habit of focusing on God's priorities and your possibilities. When you do, you'll spend less time fretting about your challenges and more time praising God for His gifts.

So today and every day hereafter, pray for a sense of balance and perspective. And remember: your thoughts are intensely powerful things, so handle them with care.

Attitude is the mind's paintbrush;
it can color any situation.

———

Barbara Johnson

Instead of being frustrated and overwhelmed by all that is going on in our world, go to the Lord and ask Him to give you His eternal perspective.

Kay Arthur

People who do not develop and practice good thinking often find themselves at the mercy of their circumstances.

John Maxwell

All I'm doing right now, friends, is showing how these things pertain to Apollos and me so that you will learn restraint and not rush into making judgments without knowing all the facts. It is important to look at things from God's point of view. I would rather not see you inflating or deflating reputations based on mere hearsay.

1 Corinthians 4:6 MSG

Today's Prayer

Dear Lord, when the pace of my life becomes frantic, slow me down and give me perspective. Give me the wisdom to realize that the problems of today are only temporary but that Your love is eternal. When I become discouraged, keep me steady and sure, so that I might do Your will here on earth and then live with You forever in heaven. Amen

Time to Praise God

*I will praise you, Lord, with all my heart. I will tell all
the miracles you have done. I will be happy because of you;
God Most High, I will sing praises to your name.*
Psalm 9:1-2 NCV

When is the best time to praise God? In church?
Before dinner is served? When we tuck little
children into bed? None of the above. The
best time to praise God is all day, every day, to the greatest
extent we can, with thanksgiving in our hearts.

Too many of us, even well-intentioned believers,
tend to "compartmentalize" our waking hours into a
few familiar categories: work, rest, play, family time, and
worship. To do so is a mistake. Worship and praise should
be woven into the fabric of everything we do; it should
never be relegated to a weekly three-hour visit to church
on Sunday morning.

Mrs. Charles E. Cowman, the author of the classic
devotional text *Streams in the Desert*, wrote, "Two wings
are necessary to lift our souls toward God: prayer and
praise. Prayer asks. Praise accepts the answer." Today, find
a little more time to lift your concerns to God in prayer,

and praise Him for all that He has done. He's listening . . .
and He wants to hear from you.

Nothing we do is more powerful or more life-changing
than praising God.

Stormie Omartian

Praise opens the window of our hearts, preparing us to
walk more closely with God. Prayer raises the window of
our spirit, enabling us to listen more clearly to the Father.

Max Lucado

*Therefore, through Him let us continually offer up to God a
sacrifice of praise, that is, the fruit of our lips that confess His
name.*

Hebrews 13:15 HCSB

Today's Prayer

Heavenly Father, I come to You today with hope in my
heart and praise on my lips. Make me a faithful steward of
the blessings You have entrusted to me. Let me follow in
Christ's footsteps today and every day that I live. And let
my words and deeds praise You now and forever. Amen

God's Abundance

I came that they may have life,
and have it abundantly.

John 10:10 NASB

A re you the kind of parent who accepts God's spiritual abundance without reservation? If so, you are availing yourself of the peace and the joy that He has promised. Do you sincerely seek the riches that our Savior offers to those who give themselves to Him? Then follow Him. When you do, you will receive the love and the abundance that Jesus offers to those who follow Him.

Seek first the salvation that is available through a personal, passionate relationship with Christ, and then claim the joy, the peace, and the spiritual abundance that the Shepherd offers His sheep.

If we were given all we wanted here, our hearts would settle for this world rather than the next.

Elisabeth Elliot

Jesus intended for us to be overwhelmed by the blessings of regular days. He said it was the reason he had come: "I am come that they might have life, and that they might have it more abundantly."

Gloria Gaither

And God is able to make all grace abound toward you, that you, always having all sufficiency in all things, may have an abundance for every good work.

2 Corinthians 9:8 NKJV

Today's Prayer

Thank You, Dear Lord, for the abundant life that is mine through Your Son Jesus. In all that I say and do, let me share Your message of abundance with my family, my friends, and my community. Give me courage, Lord, to claim the spiritual riches that You have promised, and help me to share Your abundance with all who cross my path. Amen

The Search for Purpose

You will show me the path of life;
in Your presence is fullness of joy;
at Your right hand are pleasures forevermore.
Psalm 16:11 NKJV

L ife is best lived on purpose. And purpose, like everything else in the universe, begins with God. Whether you realize it or not, God has a plan for your life and your family, a divine calling, a direction in which He is leading you. When you welcome God into your heart and establish a genuine relationship with Him, He will begin, in time, to make His purposes known.

Sometimes, God's intentions will be clear to you; other times, God's plan will seem uncertain at best. But even on those difficult days when you are unsure which way to turn, you must never lose sight of these overriding facts: God created you for a reason; He has important work for you to do; and He's waiting patiently for you to do it.

And the next step is up to you.

When God speaks to you through the Bible, prayer, circumstances, the church, or in some other way, he has a purpose in mind for your life.

Henry Blackaby and Claude King

Oh Lord, let me not live to be useless.

John Wesley

God never calls without enabling us. In other words, if he calls you to do something, he makes it possible for you to do it.

Luci Swindoll

For everything, absolutely everything, above and below, visible and invisible, rank after rank after rank of angels—everything got started in him and finds its purpose in him.

Colossians 1:16 MSG

Today's Prayer

Dear Lord, let Your purposes be my purposes. Let Your priorities be my priorities. Let Your will be my will. Let Your Word be my guide. And, let me grow in faith and in wisdom today and every day. Amen

Making Time for Family

We can't afford to waste a minute, must not squander these
precious daylight hours in frivolity and indulgence,
in sleeping around and dissipation, in bickering and grabbing
everything in sight. Get out of bed and get dressed!
Don't loiter and linger, waiting until the very last minute.
Dress yourselves in Christ, and be up and about!
Romans 13:13-14 MSG

As every parent knows, time is a scarce commodity. There simply isn't enough time to do everything on most families' "to do" lists. That's why thoughtful parents are careful about the way that they organize and spend the time that God has given them. Wise parents carve out plenty of time to spend with spouses, kids, grandparents, siblings, and cousins.

Time is a nonrenewable gift from the Creator. But sometimes, we treat our time here on earth as if it were not a gift at all: We may be tempted to invest our lives in petty diversions or in trivial pursuits. But our Father in heaven beckons each of us to a higher calling.

It takes time to build strong family ties . . . lots of time. Yet we live in a world where time seems to be an ever-shrinking commodity as we rush from place to place with seldom a moment to spare. Has the busy pace of life robbed you of sufficient time with your loved ones? If so, it's time to fine-tune your priorities. And God can help.

When you make God a full partner in every aspect of your life, He will lead you along the proper path: His path. When you allow God to reign over your life, He will enrich your relationships and your life. So, as you plan for the day ahead, make God's priorities your priorities. When you do, every other priority will have a tendency to fall neatly into place.

The more time you give to something, the more you reveal its importance and value to you.

—

Rick Warren

What really builds togetherness is time spent together—lots of time.

Dennis Swanberg

I don't buy the cliché that quality time is the most important thing. If you don't have enough quantity, you won't get quality.

Leighton Ford

As we surrender the use of our time to the lordship of Christ, He will lead us to use it in the most productive way imaginable.

Charles Stanley

So teach us to number our days, that we may gain a heart of wisdom.

Psalm 90:12 NKJV

Today's Prayer

Dear Lord, You have given me a wonderful gift: time here on earth. Let me use it wisely—for the glory of Your kingdom and the betterment of my family—today and every day that I live. Amen

Wisdom Now!

Do you want to be counted wise, to build a reputation
for wisdom? Here's what you do:
Live well, live wisely, live humbly.
It's the way you live, not the way you talk, that counts.

James 3:13 MSG

D o you seek wisdom for yourself and for your family? Of course you do. But as a savvy parent, you know that wisdom can be an elusive commodity in today's troubled world. In a society filled with temptations and distractions; it's easy for parents and children alike to stray far from the source of the ultimate wisdom: God's Holy Word.

When you begin a daily study of God's Word and live according to His commandments, you will become wise . . . in time. But don't expect to open your Bible today and be wise tomorrow. Wisdom is not like a mushroom; it does not spring up overnight. It is, instead, like an oak tree that starts as a tiny acorn, grows into a sapling, and eventually reaches up to the sky, tall and strong.

Today and every day, as a way of understanding God's plan for your life, study His Word and live by it. When you do, you will accumulate a storehouse of wisdom that will enrich your own life and the lives of your family members, your friends, and the world.

The more wisdom enters our hearts, the more we will be able to trust our hearts in difficult situations.

John Eldredge

If you lack knowledge, go to school. If you lack wisdom, get on your knees.

Vance Havner

Don't turn your back on wisdom, for she will protect you. Love her, and she will guard you.

Proverbs 4:6 NLT

Today's Prayer

Dear Lord, give me wisdom to love my family, to care for them, and to help them understand the wisdom of Your Holy Word. Let me share Your wisdom by the words I speak and the example that I set, today and every day that I live. Amen

Getting the Work Done

Do not be lazy but work hard,
serving the Lord with all your heart.
Romans 12:11 NCV

The world often promises instant gratification: Get rich—today. Lose weight—this week. Have whatever you want—right now. Yet life's experiences and God's Word teach us that the best things in life require heaping helpings of both time and work.

It has been said, quite correctly, that there are no shortcuts to any place worth going. So it's important to remember that hard work is not simply a proven way to get ahead; it's also part of God's plan.

Today, do yourself this favor: Don't look for shortcuts (because there aren't any) and don't expect easy solutions to life's big challenges (because big rewards usually require lots of effort). You and your loved ones inhabit a world in which instant gratification is rare, but the rewards of hard work are not. Shape your expectations—and your work habits—accordingly.

God does not want us to work for Him, nor does He want to be our helper. Rather, He wants to do His work in and through us.

Vonette Bright

People who work for money only are usually miserable, because there is no fulfillment and no meaning to what they do.

Dave Ramsey

Ordinary work, which is what most of us do most of the time, is ordained by God every bit as much as is the extraordinary.

Elisabeth Elliot

In all the work you are doing, work the best you can. Work as if you were doing it for the Lord, not for people.

Colossians 3:23 NCV

Today's Prayer

Lord, let me be an industrious worker in Your fields. Those fields are ripe, Lord, and Your workers are few. Let me be counted as Your faithful, diligent servant today, and every day. Amen

Beyond Worry

Let not your heart be troubled;
you believe in God, believe also in Me.
John 14:1 NKJV

B ecause you and your family members have the ability to think, you also have the ability to worry. Even if you're a very faithful Christians, you may be plagued by occasional periods of discouragement and doubt. Even though you trust God's promise of salvation— even though you sincerely believe in God's love and protection—you may find yourself upset by the countless details of everyday life.

Where is the best place to take your worries? Take them to God. Take your troubles to Him; take your fears to Him; take your doubts to Him; take your weaknesses to Him; take your sorrows to Him . . . and leave them all there. Seek protection from the One who offers you eternal salvation—build your spiritual house upon the Rock that cannot be moved.

Perhaps you or your loved ones are concerned about the future or about your relationships or about your finances. Or perhaps you are simply "worriers" by nature. If so, remember that God still sits in His heaven and that you are His beloved children. Then, perhaps, you will worry a little less and trust God a little more, and that's as it should be because God is trustworthy . . . and you are protected.

Today is mine.
Tomorrow is none of my business.
If I peer anxiously into the fog of the future,
I will strain my spiritual eyes
so that I will not see clearly
what is required of me now.

—

Elisabeth Elliot

The beginning of anxiety is the end of faith, and the beginning of true faith is the end of anxiety.

George Mueller

Much that worries us beforehand can, quite unexpectedly, have a happy and simple solution. Worries just don't matter. Things really are in a better hand than ours.

Dietrich Bonhoeffer

God is bigger than your problems. Whatever worries press upon you today, put them in God's hands and leave them there.

Billy Graham

Trust in him at all times, O people; pour out your hearts to him, for God is our refuge.

Psalm 62:8 NIV

Today's Prayer

Dear Lord, wherever I find myself, let me celebrate more and worry less. When my faith begins to waver, help me to trust You more. Then, with praise on my lips and the love of Your Son in my heart, let me live courageously, faithfully, prayerfully, and thankfully this day and every day. Amen

Family Worship

Worship the Lord with gladness. Come before him,
singing with joy. Acknowledge that the Lord is God!
He made us, and we are his.
We are his people, the sheep of his pasture.

Psalm 100:2-3 NLT

All of mankind is engaged in worship . . . of one kind or another. The question is not whether we worship, but what we worship. Some of us choose to worship God. The result is a plentiful harvest of joy, peace, and abundance. Others distance themselves from God by foolishly worshiping things of this earth such as fame, fortune, or personal gratification. To do so is a terrible mistake with eternal consequences.

Whenever we place our love for material possessions above our love for God—or when we yield to the countless temptations of this world—we find ourselves engaged in a struggle between good and evil, a clash between God and Satan. Our responses to these struggles have implications that echo throughout our families and throughout our communities.

How can we ensure that we cast our lot with God? We do so, in part, by the practice of regular, purposeful worship with our families. When we worship God faithfully and fervently, we are blessed. When we fail to worship God, for whatever reason, we forfeit the spiritual gifts that He intends for us.

We must worship our Heavenly Father, not just with our words, but also with deeds. We must honor Him, praise Him, and obey Him. As we seek to find purpose and meaning for our lives, we must first seek His purpose and His will. For believers, God comes first. Always first.

> Worship is our response to the overtures of love from the heart of the Father.
>
> — Richard Foster

Because his spiritual existence transcends form, matter, and location, we have the freedom to worship him and experience his indwelling presence wherever we are.

R. C. Sproul

God asks that we worship Him with our concentrated minds as well as with our wills and emotions. A divided and scattered mind is not effective.

Catherine Marshall

But an hour is coming, and is now here, when the true worshipers will worship the Father in spirit and truth. Yes, the Father wants such people to worship Him. God is Spirit, and those who worship Him must worship in spirit and truth.

John 4:23-24 HCSB

Today's Prayer

Heavenly Father, let today and every day be a time of worship for my family and me. Let us worship You, not only with words but also with deeds. In the quiet moments of the day, let us praise You and thank You for creating us, loving us, guiding us, and saving us. Amen

Accepting Life

The Lord says, "Forget what happened before,
and do not think about the past. Look at the new thing
I am going to do. It is already happening. Don't you see it?
I will make a road in the desert and rivers in the dry land."

Isaiah 43:18-19 NCV

Can you find the courage to accept the past by forgiving all those who have injured you (including yourself)? If you can, you can then look to the future with a sense of optimism and hope.

God has instructed you to place your hopes in Him, and He has promised that you will be His throughout eternity. Your task, as a positive role model for—and a concerned leader of—your family, is to take God at His word.

Of course, we all face occasional disappointments and failures while we are here on earth, but these are only temporary defeats. Of course, this world can be a place of trials and tribulations, but we are secure. God has promised us peace, joy, and eternal life. And God keeps His promises today, tomorrow, and forever.

Trust the past to God's mercy,
the present to God's love,
and the future
to God's providence.

—

St. Augustine

Surrender to the Lord is not a tremendous sacrifice, not an agonizing performance. It is the most sensible thing you can do.

Corrie ten Boom

Acceptance is taking from God's hand absolutely anything He gives, looking into His face in trust and thanksgiving, knowing that the confinement of the situation we're in is good and for His glory.

Charles Swindoll

Should we accept only good things from the hand of God and never anything bad?

Job 2:10 NLT

Today's Prayer

Dear Lord, let me live in the present, not the past. Let me focus on my blessings, not my sorrows. Give me the wisdom to be thankful for the gifts that I do have, and not bitter about the things that I don't have. Let me accept what was, let me give thanks for what is, and let me have faith in what most surely will be: the promise of eternal life with You. Amen

Day 71

Getting It Done Now

*When you make a vow to God, don't delay fulfilling it,
because He does not delight in fools. Fulfill what you vow.*
Ecclesiastes 5:4 HCSB

The old saying is both familiar and true: actions speak louder than words. And as Christian parents, we must beware: our actions should always give credence to the changes that Christ can make in the lives of those who walk with Him.

God calls upon each of us to act in accordance with His will and with respect for His commandments. If we are to be responsible believers, we must realize that it is never enough simply to hear the instructions of God; we must also live by them. And it is never enough to wait idly by while others do God's work here on earth; we, too, must act. Doing God's work is a responsibility that each of us must bear, and when we do, our loving Heavenly Father rewards our efforts with a bountiful harvest.

Do noble things, do not dream them all day long.

Charles Kingsley

Now is the only time worth having because, indeed, it is the only time we have.

C. H. Spurgeon

Every time you refuse to face up to life and its problems, you weaken your character.

E. Stanley Jones

We spend our lives dreaming of the future, not realizing that a little of it slips away every day.

Barbara Johnson

For the Kingdom of God is not just fancy talk; it is living by God's power.

1 Corinthians 4:20 NLT

Today's Prayer

Dear Lord, today is a new day. Help me tackle the important tasks immediately, even if those tasks are unpleasant. Don't let me put off until tomorrow what I should do today. Amen

Behaving Differently

So don't get tired of doing what is good.
Don't get discouraged and give up,
for we will reap a harvest of blessing at the appropriate time.
Galatians 6:9 NLT

Oswald Chambers, the author of the Christian classic *My Utmost for His Highest*, advised, "Never support an experience which does not have God as its source, and faith in God as its result." These words serve as a powerful reminder that, as Christian parents, we are called to walk with God and obey His commandments. But, we live in a world that presents countless temptations for adults and even more temptations for our children.

We Christians, when confronted with sin, have clear instructions: walk—or better yet run—in the opposite direction. When we do, we reap the blessings that God has promised to all those who live according to His will and His word.

Although God causes all things to work together for good for His children, He still holds us accountable for our behavior.

Kay Arthur

Either God's Word keeps you from sin, or sin keeps you from God's Word.

Corrie ten Boom

There may be no trumpet sound or loud applause when we make a right decision, just a calm sense of resolution and peace.

Gloria Gaither

The purity of motive determines the quality of action.

Oswald Chambers

In everything set them an example by doing what is good.

Titus 2:7 NIV

Today's Prayer

Lord, there is a right way and a wrong way to live. Let me live according to Your rules, not the world's rules. Your path is right for my family and me. Let us follow Your path, Father, every day of our lives. Amen

Discipline Now

It is better to be patient than powerful;
it is better to have self-control than to conquer a city.
Proverbs 16:32 NLT

Parents who study the Bible are confronted again and again with God's intention that His children (of all ages) lead disciplined lives. God doesn't reward laziness or misbehavior. To the contrary, He expects His followers to adopt a disciplined approach to their lives, and He punishes those who disobey His commandments. So, wise Christian parents teach discipline by word and by example, but not necessarily in that order.

As we seek to become disciples of Jesus Christ, we should never forget that the word *disciple* is directly related to the word *discipline*. To be a disciple of the Lord Jesus Christ is to know His discipline.

God does not discipline out of anger; His discipline is not like human wrath. God always disciplines out of love, and as parents we should do likewise.

When you find the need to discipline your child, as you most certainly will from time to time, do so lovingly, not angrily. And remember that the greatest rewards in life usually accrue to the children who are lucky enough to have parents who care enough to give their kids the benefit of a disciplined, loving home.

If one examines the secret behind a championship football team, a magnificent orchestra, or a successful business, the principal ingredient is invariably discipline.

James Dobson

Personal humility is a spiritual discipline and the hallmark of the service of Jesus.

Franklin Graham

But I discipline my body and bring it into subjection, lest, when I have preached to others, I myself should become disqualified.

1 Corinthians 9:27 NKJV

Today's Prayer

Lord, let me be a disciplined parent, and let me teach my children to lead disciplined lives. Let me be Your faithful servant, and let me teach faithfulness by my conduct and by my communications. Let me raise my family in the knowledge of Your Word, Father, and let me follow Your commandments just as surely as I teach my children to obey You and to love You. Amen

Choices

I am offering you life or death, blessings or curses.
Now, choose life! . . . To choose life is to love
the Lord your God, obey him, and stay close to him.
Deuteronomy 30:19-20 NCV

Life is a series of decisions and choices. Each day, we make countless decisions that can bring us closer to God . . . or not. When we live according to God's commandments, we earn for ourselves the abundance and peace that He intends for our lives. But, when we turn our backs upon God by disobeying Him, we bring needless suffering upon ourselves and our families.

Do you seek spiritual abundance that can be yours through the person of God's only begotten Son? Then invite Christ into your heart and live according to His teachings. And, when you confront a difficult decision or a powerful temptation, seek God's wisdom and trust it. When you do, you will receive untold blessings—not only for this day, but also for all eternity.

Life is a series of choices between the bad, the good, and the best. Everything depends on how we choose.

Vance Havner

Every day, I find countless opportunities to decide whether I will obey God and demonstrate my love for Him or try to please myself or the world system. God is waiting for my choices.

Bill Bright

We are either the masters or the victims of our attitudes. It is a matter of personal choice. Who we are today is the result of choices we made yesterday. Tomorrow, we will become what we choose today. To change means to choose to change.

John Maxwell

The thing you should want most is God's kingdom and doing what God wants. Then all these other things you need will be given to you.

Matthew 6:33 NCV

Today's Prayer

Heavenly Father, I have many choices to make. Help me choose wisely as I follow in the footsteps of Your only begotten Son. Amen

You and Your Conscience

*If the way you live isn't consistent with what you believe,
then it's wrong.*

Romans 14:23 MSG

Billy Graham correctly observed, "Most of us follow our conscience as we follow a wheelbarrow. We push it in front of us in the direction we want to go." To do so, of course, is a profound mistake. Yet all of us, on occasion, have failed to listen to the voice that God planted in our hearts, and all of us have suffered the consequences.

God gave you a conscience for a very good reason: to make your path conform to His will. Wise believers make it a practice to listen carefully to that quiet internal voice. Count yourself among that number. When your conscience speaks, listen and learn. In all likelihood, God is trying to get His message through. And in all likelihood, it is a message that you desperately need to hear.

To go against one's conscience is neither safe nor right. Here I stand. I cannot do otherwise.

Martin Luther

The convicting work of the Holy Spirit awakens, disturbs, and judges.

Franklin Graham

God desires that we become spiritually healthy enough through faith to have a conscience that rightly interprets the work of the Holy Spirit.

Beth Moore

So I strive always to keep my conscience clear before God and man.

Acts 24:16 NIV

Today's Prayer

Dear Lord, You speak to me through the gift of Your Holy Word. And, Father, You speak to me through that still small voice that tells me right from wrong. Let me follow Your way, Lord, and, in these quiet moments, show me Your plan for this day, that I might serve You. Amen

Genuine Contentment

I have learned to be content
in whatever circumstances I am.
Philippians 4:11 HCSB

The preoccupation with happiness and contentment is an ever-present theme in the modern world. We are bombarded with messages that tell us where to find peace and pleasure in a world that worships materialism and wealth. But, lasting contentment is not found in material possessions; genuine contentment is a spiritual gift from God to those who trust in Him and follow His commandments.

Where can you and your family members find contentment? If you don't find it in God, you will never find it anywhere else. But, if you put your faith and your trust in Him, you will be blessed with an inner peace that is beyond human understanding. When God dwells at the center of your lives, peace and contentment will belong to you just as surely as you belong to God.

He is truly happy who has all that he wishes to have, and wishes to have nothing that he ought not to have.

St. Augustine

Contentment is not escape from battle, but rather an abiding peace and confidence in the midst of battle.

Warren Wiersbe

I believe that in every time and place it is within our power to acquiesce in the will of God—and what peace it brings to do so!

Elisabeth Elliot

But godliness with contentment is a great gain.

1 Timothy 6:6 HCSB

Today's Prayer

Dear Lord, let me strive to do Your will here on earth, and as I do, let me find contentment and balance. Let me live in the light of Your will and Your priorities for my life. And let me teach my children the peace and contentment that can be theirs through the gift of Your Son. Amen

Your Noisy World

*Be silent before the Lord
and wait expectantly for Him.*
Psalm 37:7 HCSB

Face it: We live in a noisy world, a world filled with distractions, frustrations, and complications. But if we allow those distractions to separate us from God's peace, we do ourselves a profound disservice.

Are you one of those busy parents who rush through the day with scarcely a single moment for quiet contemplation and prayer? If so, it's time to reorder your priorities.

Nothing is more important than the time you spend with your Savior. So be still and claim the inner peace that is your spiritual birthright: the peace of Jesus Christ. It is offered freely; it has been paid for in full; it is yours for the asking. So ask. And then share.

Growth takes place in quietness, in hidden ways, in silence and solitude. The process is not accessible to observation.

Eugene Peterson

The manifold rewards of a serious, consistent prayer life demonstrate clearly that time with our Lord should be our first priority.

Shirley Dobson

The Lord Jesus, available to people much of the time, left them, sometimes a great while before day, to go up to the hills where He could commune in solitude with His Father.

Elisabeth Elliot

In quietness and confidence shall be your strength.

Isaiah 30:15 NKJV

Today's Prayer

Lord, Your Holy Word is a light unto the world; let me study it, trust it, and share it with all who cross my path. Let me discover You, Father, in the quiet moments of the day. And, in all that I say and do, help me to be a worthy witness as I share the Good News of Your perfect Son and Your perfect Word. Amen

Running on Empty?

I will give you a new heart and put a new spirit in you . . . .
Ezekiel 36:26 NIV

God intends that His children lead joyous lives filled with abundance and peace. But sometimes, as all parents can attest, abundance and peace seem very far away. It is then that we must turn to God for renewal, and when we do, He will restore us.

Have you "tapped in" to the power of God, or are you muddling along under your own power? If you are weary, worried, fretful, or fearful, then it is time to turn to a strength much greater than your own.

The Bible tells us that we can do all things through the power of our risen Savior, Jesus Christ. Our challenge, then, is clear: we must place Christ where He belongs: at the very center of our lives.

Are you tired or troubled? Turn your heart toward God in prayer. Are you weak or worried? Make the time to delve deeply into God's Holy Word. When you do, you'll discover that the Creator of the universe stands ready and able to create a new sense of wonderment and joy in you.

If you're willing to repair your life, God is willing to help. If you're not willing to repair your life, God is willing to wait.

Marie T. Freeman

He is the God of wholeness and restoration.

Stormie Omartian

Satan does some of his worst work on exhausted Christians when nerves are frayed and the mind is faint.

Vance Havner

The One who was sitting on the throne said, "Look! I am making everything new!" Then he said, "Write this, because these words are true and can be trusted."

Revelation 21:5 NCV

Today's Prayer

Lord, I am an imperfect parent. Sometimes, I become overwhelmed by the demands of the day. When I feel tired or discouraged, renew my strength. When I am worried, let me turn my thoughts and my prayers to You. Let me trust Your promises, Dear Lord, and let me accept Your unending love, now and forever. Amen

Day 79

The Spiritual Journey

*Grow in grace and understanding of our Master and Savior,
Jesus Christ. Glory to the Master, now and forever! Yes!*
2 Peter 3:18 MSG

The journey toward spiritual maturity lasts a lifetime: As Christian parents, we can and should continue to grow in the love and the knowledge of our Savior as long as we live. When we cease to grow, either emotionally or spiritually, we do ourselves and our loved ones a profound disservice. But, if we study God's Word, if we obey His commandments, and if we live in the center of His will, we will not be "stagnant" believers; we will, instead, be growing Christians . . . and that's exactly what God wants for our lives.

Many of life's most important lessons are painful to learn. During times of heartbreak and hardship, God stands ready to protect us. As Psalm 147 promises, "He heals the brokenhearted and bandages their wounds" (NCV). In His own time and according to His master plan, God will heal us if we invite Him into our hearts.

Spiritual growth need not take place only in times of adversity. We should seek to grow in our relationship with the Lord through every season of our lives, through happy times and hard times, through times of celebration and times of pain.

In those quiet moments when we open our hearts to God, the One who made us keeps remaking us. He gives us direction, perspective, wisdom, and courage. And of course, the appropriate moment to accept those spiritual gifts is always the present one.

There is wonderful freedom and joy in coming to recognize that the fun is in the becoming.

Gloria Gaither

For this reason also, since the day we heard this, we haven't stopped praying for you. We are asking that you may be filled with the knowledge of His will in all wisdom and spiritual understanding.

Colossians 1:9 HCSB

Today's Prayer

Dear Lord, the Bible tells me that You are at work in my life, continuing to help me grow and to mature in my faith. Show me Your wisdom, Father, and let me live according to Your Word and Your will. Amen

The Rewards of Discipline

God hasn't invited us into a disorderly,
unkempt life but into something holy and beautiful—
as beautiful on the inside as the outside.
1 Thessalonians 4:7 MSG

Wise parents teach their children the importance of discipline using their words and their examples. Disciplined moms and dads understand that God doesn't reward laziness or misbehavior. To the contrary, God expects His believers to lead lives that are above reproach. And, He punishes those who disobey His commandments.

It has been said that there are no shortcuts to any place worth going. Thoughtful parents agree. In Proverbs 28:19, God's message is clear: "He who works his land will have abundant food, but the one who chases fantasies will have his fill of poverty" (NIV).

When we work diligently and consistently, we can expect a bountiful harvest. But we must never expect the harvest to precede the labor. First, we must lead lives of discipline and obedience; then, we will reap the never-ending rewards that God has promised.

Real freedom means to welcome
the responsibility it brings,
to welcome the God-control
it requires, to welcome
the discipline that results,
to welcome the maturity it creates.

—

Eugenia Price

If I could just hang in there, being faithful to my own tasks, God would make me joyful and content. The responsibility is mine, but the power is His.

Peg Rankin

Discipline is training that develops and corrects.

Charles Stanley

As we seek to become disciples of Jesus Christ, we should never forget that the word *disciple* is directly related to the word *discipline*. To be a disciple of the Lord Jesus Christ is to know His discipline.

Dennis Swanberg

Discipline yourself for the purpose of godliness.

1 Timothy 4:7 NASB

Today's Prayer

Lord, let me be a disciplined parent, and let me teach my children to lead disciplined lives. Let me be Your faithful servant, Lord, and let me teach faithfulness by my conduct and by my communications. Let me raise my family in the knowledge of Your Word, and let me follow Your commandments just as surely as I teach my children to obey You and to love You. Amen

---

Saying "Thanks" to God

*Give thanks in all circumstances;
for this is God's will for you in Christ Jesus.*
1 Thessalonians 5:18 NIV

The words of 1 Thessalonians 5:18 remind us to give thanks in every circumstance of life. But sometimes, when our hearts are troubled and our spirits are crushed, we don't feel like celebrating. Yet even when the clouds of despair darken our lives, God offers us His love, His strength, and His grace. And as believers, we must thank Him.

Have you thanked God today for blessings that are too numerous to count? Have you offered Him your heartfelt prayers and your wholehearted praise? If not, it's time to slow down and to offer a prayer of thanksgiving to the One who has given you life on earth and life eternal.

No matter our circumstances, we owe God so much more than we can ever repay, and the least we can do is to thank Him.

It is only with gratitude
that life becomes rich.

—

Dietrich Bonhoeffer

We ought to give thanks for all fortune: if it is good, because it is good, if bad, because it works in us patience, humility, and the contempt of this world along with the hope of our eternal country.

C. S. Lewis

The words "thank" and "think" come from the same root word. If we would think more, we would thank more.

Warren Wiersbe

It is always possible to be thankful for what is given rather than to complain about what is not given. One or the other becomes a habit of life.

Elisabeth Elliot

Give thanks to the Lord, for He is good; His faithful love endures forever.

Psalm 118:29 HCSB

Today's Prayer

Lord, You have blessed me with a loving family—make me a parent who is thankful, loving, responsible, and wise. I praise You, Father, for the gift of Your Son and for the gift of salvation. Let me be a joyful Christian and a worthy example, this day and every day that I live. Amen

Trust the Shepherd

The Lord is my shepherd; I shall not want.
Psalm 23:1 KJV

I n the 23rd Psalm, David teaches us that God is like a watchful shepherd caring for His flock. No wonder these verses have provided comfort and hope for generations of believers.

You are precious in the eyes of God. You are His priceless creation, made in His image, and protected by Him. God watches over every step you make and every breath you take, so you need never be afraid. But sometimes, fear has a way of slipping into the minds and hearts of even the most devout believers—and you are no exception.

As a busy parent, you know from firsthand experience that life is not always easy. But as a recipient of God's grace, you also know that you are protected by a loving Heavenly Father.

On occasion, you will confront circumstances that trouble you to the very core of your soul. When you are afraid, trust in God. When you are worried, turn your concerns over to Him. When you are anxious, be still and listen for the quiet assurance of God's promises. And then, place your life in His hands. He is your shepherd today and throughout eternity. Trust the Shepherd.

Christ reigns in his church as shepherd-king. He has supremacy, but it is the superiority of a wise and tender shepherd over His needy and loving flock. He commands and receives obedience, but it is willing obedience of well-cared-for-sheep, offered joyfully to their beloved Shepherd, whose voice they know so well. He rules by the force of love and the energy of goodness.

C. H. Spurgeon

For the Lord God is our light and our protector. He gives us grace and glory. No good thing will the Lord withhold from those who do what is right. O Lord Almighty, happy are those who trust in you.

Psalm 84:11-12 NLT

Today's Prayer

Lord, You are my Shepherd. You care for me; You comfort me; You watch over me; and You have saved me. I will praise You, Father, for Your glorious works, for Your protection, for Your love, and for Your Son. Amen

Real Repentance

The one who conceals his sins will not prosper,
but whoever confesses and renounces them will find mercy.
Proverbs 28:13 HCSB

Who among us has sinned? All of us. But, God calls upon us to turn away from sin by following His commandments. And the good news is this: When we do ask God's forgiveness and turn our hearts to Him, He forgives us absolutely and completely.

Genuine repentance requires more than simply offering God apologies for our misdeeds. Real repentance may start with feelings of sorrow and remorse, but it ends only when we turn away from the sin that has heretofore distanced us from our Creator. In truth, we offer our most meaningful apologies to God not with our words but with our actions. As long as we are still engaged in sin, we may be "repenting," but we have not fully "repented."

Is there an aspect of your life that is distancing you from your God? If so, ask for His forgiveness, and—just as importantly—stop sinning. Then, wrap yourself in the protection of God's Word. When you do, you will be secure.

But suppose we do sin. Suppose we slip and fall. Suppose we yield to temptation for a moment. What happens? We have to confess that sin.

Billy Graham

Repentance begins with confession of our guilt and recognition that our sin is against God.

Charles Stanley

When true repentance comes, God will not hesitate for a moment to forgive, cast the sins in the sea of forgetfulness, and put the child on the road to restoration.

Beth Moore

Come back to the LORD and live!

Amos 5:6 NLT

Today's Prayer

When I stray from Your commandments, Lord, I must not only confess my sins, I must also turn from them. When I fall short, help me to change. When I reject Your Word and Your will for my life, guide me back to Your side. Forgive my sins, Dear Lord, and help me live according to Your plan for my life. Your plan is perfect, Father; I am not. Let me trust in You. Amen

Doing the Right Thing

The righteous one will live by his faith.
Habakkuk 2:4 HCSB

God has given us a guidebook for righteous living called the Holy Bible. It contains thorough instructions which, if followed, lead to fulfillment, righteousness, and salvation. But, if we choose to ignore God's commandments, the results are as predictable as they are tragic.

The Bible instructs us that a righteous life has many components: faith, honesty, generosity, love, kindness, humility, gratitude, and worship, to name but a few. And, if we seek to follow the steps of our Savior, Jesus Christ, we must, to the best of our abilities, live according to the principles contained in God's Holy Word.

As a loving parent, you are keenly aware that God has entrusted you with a profound responsibility: caring for the needs of your family, including their spiritual needs. To fulfill that responsibility, you must study God's Word and live by it. When you do, your example will be a blessing not only to your loved ones, but also to generations yet unborn.

Righteousness comes only from God.

Kay Arthur

If we have the true love of God in our hearts, we will show it in our lives. We will not have to go up and down the earth proclaiming it. We will show it in everything we say or do.

D. L. Moody

Holiness is not an impossibility for any of us.

Elisabeth Elliot

The purity of motive determines the quality of action.

Oswald Chambers

Lead a tranquil and quiet life in all godliness and dignity.

1 Timothy 2:2 HCSB

Today's Prayer

Dear Lord, let me obey Your Word, and let me teach my children to do the same. Make me a parent who obeys Your commandments, and let me walk righteously in the footsteps of Your Son, today and every day. Amen

A Willingness to Serve

Whoever wants to become great among you
must serve the rest of you like a servant.
Matthew 20:26 NCV

If you and your family members genuinely seek to discover God's unfolding priorities for your lives, you must ask yourselves this question: "How does God want us to serve others?" And you may be certain of this: service to others is an integral part of God's plan for your lives.

Christ was the ultimate servant, the Savior who gave His life for mankind. As His followers, we, too, must become humble servants. As Christians, we are clearly (and repeatedly) instructed to assist those in need. But, as weak human beings, we sometimes fall short as we seek to puff ourselves up and glorify our own accomplishments. Jesus commands otherwise. He teaches us that the most esteemed men and women are not the self-congratulatory leaders of society but are instead the humblest of servants.

As members of God's family, we must serve our neighbors quietly and without fanfare. We must find needs and meet them. We must lend helping hands and share kind words with humility in our hearts and praise on our lips And we must remember that every time we help someone in need, we are serving our Savior . . . which, by the way, is precisely what we must do.

———————

God does not do anything with us, only through us.

—

Oswald Chambers

Make it a rule, and pray to God to help you to keep it, never, if possible, to lie down at night without being able to say: "I have made one human being at least a little wiser, or a little happier, or at least a little better this day."

Charles Kingsley

So many times we say that we can't serve God because we aren't whatever is needed. We're not talented enough or smart enough or whatever. But if you are in covenant with Jesus Christ, He is responsible for covering your weaknesses, for being your strength. He will give you His abilities for your disabilities!

Kay Arthur

You address me as "Teacher" and "Master," and rightly so. That is what I am. So if I, the Master and Teacher, washed your feet, you must now wash each other's feet. I've laid down a pattern for you. What I've done, you do.

John 13:15 MSG

Today's Prayer

Dear Lord, when Jesus humbled Himself and became a servant, He also became an example for me. Make me a faithful steward of my gifts, and let me be a humble servant to my loved ones, to my friends, and to those in need. Amen

His Golden Rule

Do to others as you would have them do to you.
Luke 6:31 NIV

Is the Golden Rule one of the rules that governs your household? Hopefully so. Obeying the Golden Rule is a proven way to improve all your relationships, including your relationships with the people who happen to live inside the four walls of your home. But the reverse is also true: if you or your loved ones ignore the Golden Rule, you're headed for trouble, and fast.

Jesus taught us that we should treat other people (including our family members) in the same way that we want to be treated: that's the Golden Rule. Yet sometimes, especially when we're feeling pressured, tired, or upset, obeying the Golden Rule can seem like an impossible task—but it's not.

God's Word makes it clear: we are to treat our loved ones with respect, kindness, fairness, and courtesy. And He knows we can do so if we try. So if you're wondering how you should treat your loved ones—or anybody else, for that matter—just ask the person you see every time you look into the mirror. The answer you receive will tell you exactly what to do.

When you extend hospitality
to others, you're not
trying to impress people,
you're trying to
reflect God to them.

—

Max Lucado

The mark of a Christian is that he will walk the second mile and turn the other cheek. A wise man or woman gives the extra effort, all for the glory of the Lord Jesus Christ.

John Maxwell

The Golden Rule starts at home, but it should never stop there.

Marie T. Freeman

I have discovered that when I please Christ, I end up inadvertently serving others far more effectively.

Beth Moore

Therefore, God's chosen ones, holy and loved, put on heartfelt compassion, kindness, humility, gentleness, and patience.

Colossians 3:12 HCSB

Today's Prayer

Dear Lord, the Golden Rule is not only a perfect standard to use with my friends and neighbors, it is also a guide for raising my children. Enable me to respect my children as I want them to respect me. Help me to walk in their shoes and to see life from their perspective. Help me, Father, to be a nurturing, loving parent every day that I live, and may the glory be yours. Amen

Observing the Sabbath

Remember the Sabbath day, to keep it holy.
Exodus 20:8 NKJV

When God gave Moses the Ten Commandments, it became perfectly clear that our Heavenly Father intends for us to make the Sabbath a holy day, a day for worship, for contemplation, for fellowship, and for rest. Yet we live in a seven-day-a-week world, a world that all too often treats Sunday as a regular workday.

How does your family observe the Lord's day? When church is over, do you treat Sunday like any other day of the week? If so, it's time to think long and hard about your family's schedule and your family's priorities.

Whenever we ignore God's commandments, we pay a price. So if you've been treating Sunday as just another day, it's time to break that habit. When Sunday rolls around, don't try to fill every spare moment. Take time to rest . . . Father's orders!

Worship is not taught from the pulpit. It must be learned in the heart.

Jim Elliot

There is no division into sacred and secular; it is all one great, glorious life.

Oswald Chambers

God has promised to give you all of eternity. The least you can do is give Him one day a week in return.

Marie T. Freeman

You may work for six days each week, but on the seventh day all work must come to a complete stop. It is the LORD's Sabbath day of complete rest, a holy day to assemble for worship. It must be observed wherever you live.

Leviticus 23:3 NLT

Today's Prayer

Dear Lord, I thank You for the Sabbath day, a day when my family and I can worship You and praise Your Son. We will keep the Sabbath as a holy day, a day when we can honor You. Amen

The Direction of Your Thoughts

Fix your thoughts on what is true and honorable and right.
Think about things that are pure and lovely and admirable.
Think about things that are excellent and worthy of praise.
Philippians 4:8 NLT

Thoughts are intensely powerful things. Our thoughts have the power to lift us up or drag us down; they have the power to energize us or deplete us, to inspire us to greater accomplishments or to make those accomplishments impossible.

How will you and your family members direct your thoughts today? Will you obey the words of Philippians 4:8 by dwelling upon those things that are true, honorable, and right? Or will you allow your thoughts to be hijacked by the negativity that seems to dominate our troubled world?

Are you fearful, angry, bored, or worried? Are you so preoccupied with the concerns of this day that you fail to thank God for the promise of eternity? Are you confused, bitter, or pessimistic? If so, God wants to have a little talk with you.

God intends that you experience joy and abundance, but He will not force His joy upon you; you must claim it for yourself. It's up to you and your loved ones to celebrate the life that God has given you by focusing your minds upon "whatever is commendable." So form the habit of spending more time thinking about your blessings and less time fretting about your hardships. Then, take time to thank the Giver of all things good for gifts that are, in truth, far too numerous to count.

I became aware of one very important concept
I had missed before: my attitude—
not my circumstances—
was what was making me unhappy.

—

Vonette Bright

The things we think are the things that feed our souls. If we think on pure and lovely things, we shall grow pure and lovely like them; and the converse is equally true.

Hannah Whitall Smith

Your thoughts are the determining factor as to whose mold you are conformed to. Control your thoughts and you control the direction of your life.

Charles Stanley

Every major spiritual battle is in the mind.

Charles Stanley

So prepare your minds for service and have self-control.

1 Peter 1:13 NCV

Today's Prayer

Dear Lord, I will focus on Your love, Your power, Your promises, and Your Son. When I am weak, I will turn to You for strength; when I am worried, I will turn to You for comfort; when I am troubled, I will turn to You for patience and perspective. Help me guard my thoughts, Lord, so that I may honor You this day and forever. Amen

Beyond the Mistakes

*Instead, God has chosen the world's foolish things
to shame the wise, and God has chosen
the world's weak things to shame the strong.*
1 Corinthians 1:27 HCSB

As parents, we are far from perfect. And, without question, our children are imperfect as well. Thus, we are imperfect parents raising imperfect children, and, as a result, mistakes are bound to happen.

Has someone in your family experienced a recent setback? If so, it's time to start looking for the lesson that God is trying to teach. It's time to learn what needs to be learned, change what needs to be changed, and move on.

You and your loved ones should view mistakes as opportunities to reassess God's will for your lives. And while you're at it, you should consider life's inevitable disappointments to be powerful opportunities to learn more—more about yourselves, more about your circumstances, and more about your world.

Truth will sooner come out of error than from confusion.

Francis Bacon

Lord, when we are wrong, make us willing to change; and when we are right, make us easy to live with.

Peter Marshall

I hope you don't mind me telling you all this. One can learn only by seeing one's mistakes.

C. S. Lewis

God is able to take mistakes, when they are committed to Him, and make of them something for our good and for His glory.

Ruth Bell Graham

Therefore, if anyone is in Christ, he is a new creation; the old has gone, the new has come!

2 Corinthians 5:17 NIV

Today's Prayer

Heavenly Father, I am imperfect, and I fail You in many ways. Thank You for Your forgiveness. When my children fall short of Your commandments, Lord, let me love them, let me correct them, and let me forgive them just as You have forgiven them . . . and me. Amen

---

Your Testimony

And I say to you, anyone who acknowledges Me before men,
the Son of Man will also acknowledge him
before the angels of God; but whoever denies Me
before men will be denied before the angels of God.
Luke 12:8-9 HCSB

In his second letter to Timothy, Paul offers a message to believers of every generation when he writes, "God has not given us a spirit of timidity" (1:7 NASB). Paul's meaning is crystal clear: When sharing our testimonies, we, as Christians, must be courageous, forthright, and unashamed.

We live in a world that desperately needs the healing message of Christ Jesus. Every believer, each in his or her own way, bears a personal responsibility for sharing that message. If you are a believer in Christ, you know how He has touched your heart and changed your life. Now it's your turn to share the Good News with others. And remember: today is the perfect time to share your testimony because tomorrow may quite simply be too late.

The sermon of your life in
tough times ministers to people
more powerfully than
the most eloquent speaker.

—

Bill Bright

Claim the joy that is yours. Pray. And know that your joy is used by God to reach others.

Kay Arthur

There is nothing anybody else can do that can stop God from using us. We can turn everything into a testimony.

Corrie ten Boom

Faith in small things has repercussions that ripple all the way out. In a huge, dark room a little match can light up the place.

Joni Eareckson Tada

But sanctify the Lord God in your hearts, and always be ready to give a defense to everyone who asks you a reason for the hope that is in you.

1 Peter 3:15 HCSB

Today's Prayer

Lord, the life that I live and the words that I speak will tell my family and the world how I feel about You. Today and every day, let my testimony be worthy of You. Let my words be sure and true, and let my actions point others to You. Amen

The Right Kind of Fear

The fear of the Lord is the beginning of knowledge,
but fools despise wisdom and discipline.
Proverbs 1:7 NIV

Are you a parent who possesses a healthy, fearful respect for God's power? Hopefully so. After all, God's Word teaches that the fear of the Lord is the beginning of knowledge (Proverbs 1:7).

When we fear the Creator—and when we honor Him by obeying His commandments—we receive God's approval and His blessings. But, when we ignore Him or disobey His commandments, we invite disastrous consequences.

God's hand shapes the universe, it shapes our families, and it shapes our lives. God maintains absolute sovereignty over His creation, and His power is beyond comprehension. The fear of the Lord is, indeed, the beginning of knowledge. But thankfully, once we possess a healthy, reverent fear of God, we need never be fearful of anything else.

A healthy fear of God
will do much
to deter us from sin.

—

Charles Swindoll

The remarkable thing about fearing God is that when you fear God, you fear nothing else, whereas if you do not fear God, you fear everything else.

Oswald Chambers

When true believers are awed by the greatness of God and by the privilege of becoming His children, then they become sincerely motivated, effective evangelists.

Bill Hybels

The fear of God is the death of every other fear.

C. H. Spurgeon

A simple life in the Fear-of-God is better than a rich life with a ton of headaches.

Proverbs 15:16 MSG

Today's Prayer

Dear Lord, others have expectations of me, and I have hopes and desires for my life. Lord, bring all other expectations in line with Your plans for me. May my only fear be that of displeasing the One who created me. May I obey Your commandments and seek Your will this day and every day. Amen

Embracing God's Love

Unfailing love surrounds those who trust the LORD.
Psalm 32:10 NLT

As Christian parents who have been saved by God's grace, we have a profound responsibility to educate our children in the ways of the Lord. God is a loving Father. We are God's children, and we are called upon to be faithful to Him.

When we embrace God's love, we are forever changed. When we embrace God's love, we feel differently about our neighbors, our world, and ourselves. When we embrace God's love, we tell and retell the wondrous story of His Son.

We return our Father's love by sharing it with others. We honor our Heavenly Father by obeying His commandments and sharing His Good News. When we do, we are blessed . . . and the Father smiles.

Jesus loves us with fidelity,
purity, constancy, and passion,
no matter how imperfect we are.

—

Stormie Omartian

If you have an obedience problem, you have a love problem. Focus your attention on God's love.

Henry Blackaby

Even when we cannot see the why and wherefore of God's dealings, we know that there is love in and behind them, so we can rejoice always.

J. I. Packer

The life of faith is a daily exploration of the constant and countless ways in which God's grace and love are experienced.

Eugene Peterson

We know how much God loves us, and we have put our trust in him. God is love, and all who live in love live in God, and God lives in them.

1 John 4:16 NLT

Today's Prayer

Thank You, Dear God, for Your love. You are my loving Father. I thank You for Your love and for Your Son. I will praise You; I will worship You; and, I will love You today, tomorrow, and forever. Amen

Big Plans

"I say this because I know what I am planning for you,"
says the Lord. "I have good plans for you,
not plans to hurt you. I will give you hope and a good future."
Jeremiah 29:11 NCV

God has a plan for every aspect of His creation, including your family. But He won't force His plans upon you—God has given you free will, the ability to make choices for yourselves, and once you've made those choices, you will live with the consequences.

Think about the role that God plays in the life of your family. Think about the choices you're making and how those choices may be a part of God's plan for your clan. Remember that all wisdom comes from the Creator, including the wisdom you'll need to become a world-class parent.

God intends to use you in wonderful, unexpected ways, and He seeks to do the same for your children. But make no mistake: the Father won't force you to follow His will and His path. It's up to you to seek God's plan for your life, and encourage your family to do the same. When you do, the Lord will bless you and keep you . . . today, tomorrow, and forever.

The Almighty does nothing without reason, although the frail mind of man cannot explain the reason.

St. Augustine

One of the wonderful things about being a Christian is the knowledge that God has a plan for our lives.

Warren Wiersbe

God prepared a plan for your life alone—and neither man nor the devil can destroy that plan.

Kay Arthur

Teach me to do Your will, for You are my God. May Your gracious Spirit lead me on level ground.

Psalm 143:10 HCSB

Today's Prayer

Dear Lord, I will seek Your plan for my life and my family. Even when I don't understand why things happen, I will trust You. Even when I am uncertain of my next step, I will trust You. There are many things that I cannot do, Lord, and there are many things that I cannot understand. But one thing I can do is to trust You always. And I will. Amen

He's Here

Draw near to God, and He will draw near to you.
James 4:8 HCSB

I f you are a busy parent with more obligations than you have time to count, you know all too well that the demands of everyday life can, on occasion, seem overwhelming. Thankfully, even on the days when you feel overburdened, overworked, overstressed and under-appreciated, God is trying to get His message through . . . your job is to listen.

Are you tired, discouraged, or fearful? Be comforted because God is with you. Are you confused? Listen to the quiet voice of your Heavenly Father. Are you bitter? Talk with God and seek His guidance. In whatever condition you find yourself—whether you are happy or sad, victorious or vanquished, troubled or triumphant—carve out moments of silent solitude to celebrate God's gifts and to experience His presence.

When you earnestly seek God, you will find Him because He is here, waiting patiently for you to reach out to Him . . . right here . . . right now.

Our souls were made to live in an upper atmosphere, and we stifle and choke if we live on any lower level. Our eyes were made to look off from these heavenly heights, and our vision is distorted by any lower gazing.

Hannah Whitall Smith

If you want to hear God's voice clearly and you are uncertain, then remain in His presence until He changes that uncertainty. Often, much can happen during this waiting for the Lord. Sometimes, He changes pride into humility, doubt into faith and peace.

Corrie ten Boom

Get yourself into the presence of the loving Father. Just place yourself before Him, and look up into His face; think of His love, His wonderful, tender, pitying love.

Andrew Murray

I am not alone, because the Father is with Me.

John 16:32 HCSB

Today's Prayer

Dear Lord, You are with me when I am strong and when I am weak. You never leave my side, even when it seems to me that You are far away. Today and every day, let me trust Your promises and let me feel Your love. Amen

---

He Keeps His Promises

Let us hold on to the confession of our hope without wavering,
for He who promised is faithful.

Hebrews 10:23 HCSB

God has made quite a few promises to you, and He intends to keep every single one of them. You will find these promises in a book like no other: the Holy Bible. The Bible is your roadmap for life here on earth and for life eternal—as a believer, you are called upon to trust its promises, to follow its commandments, and to share its Good News.

God has made promises to all of humanity and to you. God's promises never fail and they never grow old. You must trust those promises and share them with your family, with your friends, and with the world . . . starting now . . . and ending never.

Shake the dust from your past, and move forward in His promises.

Kay Arthur

There are four words I wish we would never forget, and they are, "God keeps His word."

Charles Swindoll

The stars may fall, but God's promises will stand and be fulfilled.

J. I. Packer

God's promises are overflowings from His great heart.

C. H. Spurgeon

As for God, his way is perfect. All the LORD's promises prove true. He is a shield for all who look to him for protection.

Psalm 18:30 NLT

Today's Prayer

Lord, Your Holy Word contains promises, and I will trust them. I will use the Bible as my guide, and I will trust You, Lord, to speak to me through Your Holy Spirit and through Your Holy Word, this day and forever. Amen

The Ultimate Protection

The Lord is my rock, my fortress, and my deliverer,
my God, my mountain where I seek refuge.
My shield, the horn of my salvation, my stronghold,
my refuge, and my Savior.
2 Samuel 22:2-3 HCSB

As a busy parent, you know from firsthand experience that life is not always easy. But as a recipient of God's grace, you also know that you are protected by a loving Heavenly Father.

In times of trouble, God will comfort you; in times of sorrow, He will dry your tears. When you are troubled, weak, or sorrowful, God is neither distant nor disinterested. To the contrary, God is always present and always vitally engaged in the events of your life. Reach out to Him, and build your future on the rock that cannot be shaken . . . trust in God and rely upon His provisions. He can provide everything you really need . . . and far, far more.

Under heaven's lock and key,
we are protected by the most
efficient security system available:
the power of God.

—

Charles Swindoll

He goes before us, follows behind us, and hems us safe inside the realm of His protection.

Beth Moore

Prayer is our pathway not only to divine protection, but also to a personal, intimate relationship with God.

Shirley Dobson

A mighty fortress is our God, a bulwark never failing / Our helper He, amid the flood of mortal ills prevailing / For still our ancient foe doth seek to work us woe / His craft and power are great, armed with cruel hate, / Our earth is not his equal.

Martin Luther

If God is for us, who is against us?

Romans 8:31 HCSB

Today's Prayer

Lord, sometimes life is difficult. Sometimes, I am worried, weary, or heartbroken. And sometimes, I encounter powerful temptations to disobey Your commandments. But, when I lift my eyes to You, Father, You strengthen me. When I am weak, You lift me up. Today, I will turn to You for strength, for hope, for direction, and for deliverance. Amen

---

Problem-solving 101

For a righteous man may fall seven times and rise again.
Proverbs 24:16 NKJV

L ife is an adventure in problem-solving. The question is not whether we will encounter problems; the real question is how we will choose to address them. When it comes to solving the problems of everyday living, we often know precisely what needs to be done, but we may be slow in doing it—especially if what needs to be done is difficult. So we put off till tomorrow what should be done today.

As a parent living here in the 21st-century, you have your own set of challenges. As you face those challenges, you may be comforted by this fact: Trouble, of every kind, is temporary. Yet God's grace is eternal. And worries, of every kind, are temporary. But God's love is everlasting. The troubles that concern you will pass. God remains. And for every problem, God has a solution.

The words of Psalm 34 remind us that the Lord solves problems for "people who do what is right." And usually, doing "what is right" means doing the uncomfortable work of confronting our problems sooner rather than later. So with no further ado, let the problem-solving begin . . . right now.

We are all faced with a series of great opportunities, brilliantly disguised as unsolvable problems. Unsolvable without God's wisdom, that is.

Charles Swindoll

Life will be made or broken at the place where we meet and deal with obstacles.

E. Stanley Jones

Each problem is a God-appointed instructor.

Charles Swindoll

Let not your heart be troubled: ye believe in God, believe also in me.

John 14:1 KJV

Today's Prayer

Lord, sometimes my problems are simply too big for me, but they are never too big for You. Let me turn my troubles over to You, Lord, and let me trust in You today and for all eternity. Amen

Considering the Cross

*But as for me, I will never boast about anything except the
cross of our Lord Jesus Christ, through whom the world has
been crucified to me, and I to the world.*
Galatians 6:14 HCSB

As we consider Christ's sacrifice on the cross, we
should be profoundly humbled and profoundly
grateful. And today, as we come to Christ
in prayer, we should do so in a spirit of quiet, heartfelt
devotion to the One who gave His life so that we might
have life eternal.

He was the Son of God, but He wore a crown of
thorns. He was the Savior of mankind, yet He was put
to death on a roughhewn cross made of wood. He offered
His healing touch to an unsaved world, and yet the same
hands that had healed the sick and raised the dead were
pierced with nails.

Christ humbled Himself on a cross—for you. He
shed His blood—for you. He has offered to walk with
you through this life and throughout all eternity. As you
approach Him today in prayer, think about His sacrifice
and His grace. And be humble.

Jesus challenges you and me to keep our focus daily on the cross of His will if we want to be His disciples.

Anne Graham Lotz

God is my Heavenly Father. He loves me with an everlasting love. The proof of that is the Cross.

Elisabeth Elliot

The cross takes care of the past. The cross takes care of the flesh. The cross takes care of the world.

Kay Arthur

I am the good shepherd. The good shepherd lays down his life for the sheep.

John 10:11 HCSB

Today's Prayer

Dear Jesus, You are my Savior and my protector. You suffered on the cross for me, and I will give You honor and praise every day of my life. I will honor You with my words, my thoughts, and my prayers. And I will live according to Your commandments, so that through me, others might come to know Your perfect love. Amen

His Commandments

Teach me Your way, O LORD;
I will walk in Your truth.
Psalm 86:11 NASB

Elisabeth Elliot advised, "Obedience to God is our job. The results of that obedience are God's." These words serve to remind us that obedience is imperative, but we live in a society that surrounds us with temptations to disobey God's laws. So if we are to win the battle against temptation and sin, we must never drop our guard.

A righteous life has many components: faith, honesty, generosity, love, kindness, humility, gratitude, and worship, to name but a few. If we seek to follow the steps of our Savior, Jesus Christ, we must seek to live according to His commandments.

When we seek righteousness in our own lives—and when we seek the companionship of like-minded friends—we not only build our characters, but we also reap the spiritual rewards that God offers those who obey Him. When we live in accordance with God's commandments, He blesses us in ways that we cannot fully understand.

Are you ready, willing, able, and anxious to receive God's blessings? Then obey Him. And rest assured that when you do your part, He'll do His part.

✦————————✦

Bible history is filled with people
who began the race with
great success but failed
at the end because
they disregarded God's rules.

—

Warren Wiersbe

The Ten Commandments were given to evoke fear and reverence for the Holy One so that obedience and blessing might result.

Beth Moore

Only grief and disappointment can result from continued violation of the divine principles that underlie the spiritual life.

A. W. Tozer

Don't worry about what you do not understand. Worry about what you do understand in the Bible but do not live by.

Corrie ten Boom

God chose you to be his people, so I urge you now to live the life to which God called you.

Ephesians 4:1 NCV

Today's Prayer

Thank You, Dear Lord, for loving me enough to give me rules to live by. Let me live by Your commandments, and let me lead others to do the same. Let me walk righteously in Your way, Dear Lord, this day and every day. Amen

The Gift of Eternal Life

For God so loved the world that he gave his only Son,
so that everyone who believes in him
will not perish but have eternal life.

John 3:16 NLT

Eternal life is not an event that begins when we die. Eternal life begins when we invite Jesus into our hearts. The moment we allow Jesus to reign over our hearts, we've already begun our eternal journeys.

As a thoughtful Christian parent, it's important to remind your child that God's plans are not limited to the ups and downs of everyday life. In fact, the ups and downs of the daily grind are, quite often, impossible for us to understand. As mere mortals, our understanding of the present and our visions for the future—like our lives here on earth—are limited. God's vision is not burdened by such limitations: His plans extend throughout all eternity. And we must trust Him even when we cannot understand the particular details of His plan.

So let us praise the Creator for His priceless gift, and let us share the Good News with all who cross our paths. We return our Father's love by accepting His grace and by sharing His message and His love. When we do, we are blessed here on earth and throughout all eternity.

The gift of God is eternal life, spiritual life, abundant life through faith in Jesus Christ, the Living Word of God.

Anne Graham Lotz

Teach us to set our hopes on heaven, to hold firmly to the promise of eternal life, so that we can withstand the struggles and storms of this world.

Max Lucado

Just then someone came up and asked Him, "Teacher, what good must I do to have eternal life?" "Why do you ask Me about what is good?" He said to him. "There is only One who is good. If you want to enter into life, keep the commandments."

Matthew 19:16-17 HCSB

Today's Prayer

Lord, I'm only here on earth for a brief visit. Heaven is my real home. You've given me the gift of eternal life through Your Son Jesus. I accept Your gift, Lord. And I will share Your Good News so that my family and friends, too, might come to know Christ's healing touch. Amen

If I speak the languages of men and of angels, but do not have love, I am a sounding gong or a clanging cymbal.
If I have the gift of prophecy, and understand all mysteries and all knowledge, and if I have all faith, so that I can move mountains, but do not have love, I am nothing.
And if I donate all my goods to feed the poor, and if I give my body to be burned, but do not have love, I gain nothing.
Love is patient; love is kind. Love does not envy; is not boastful; is not conceited; does not act improperly; is not selfish; is not provoked; does not keep a record of wrongs; finds no joy in unrighteousness, but rejoices in the truth; bears all things, believes all things, hopes all things, endures all things. Love never ends. But as for prophecies, they will come to an end; as for languages, they will cease; as for knowledge, it will come to an end. For we know in part, and we prophesy in part. But when the perfect comes, the partial will come to an end. When I was a child, I spoke like a child, I thought like a child, I reasoned like a child. When I became a man, I put aside childish things. For now we see indistinctly, as in a mirror, but then face to face. Now I know in part, but then I will know fully, as I am fully known.
Now these three remain: faith, hope, and love.
But the greatest of these is love.

—

1 Corinthians 13:1-13 HCSB